*Great
Moments
in Golf*

Bob Hope, holding the author's previous book, poses with Freddy Corcoran, Executive Director of the International Golf Association, at West Palm Beach during the National PGA Championship of 1971 where Mr. Hope was the Honorary Chairman. (Photo by Nevin H. Gibson)

Great Moments in Golf

NEVIN H. GIBSON

SOUTH BRUNSWICK AND NEW YORK:
A. S. BARNES AND COMPANY
LONDON: THOMAS YOSELOFF LTD

© 1973 by A. S. Barnes and Co., Inc.

A. S. Barnes and Co., Inc.
Cranbury, New Jersey 08512

Thomas Yoseloff Ltd
108 New Bond Street
London W1Y OQX, England

Library of Congress Cataloging in Publication Data

Gibson, Nevin H.
    Great moments in golf.

    1. Golf—Biography.   I. Title.
GV964.A1G5   796.352′092′2   79-37833
ISBN 0-498-01121-6

Other books by Nevin H. Gibson

The Encyclopedia of Golf
You Can Play Par Golf
A Pictorial History of Golf

Printed in the United States of America

Dedication

This book is affectionately and most respectfully dedicated to the late Robert Tyre Jones, Jr., whose most tremendous contribution to the Royal and Ancient Sport is indeed immeasurable.

The immortal amateur with the most impeccable swing captivated the golfing world during the "Sports Golden Decade" by winning thirteen major championships in a span of seven years.

Reaching the zenith of his fabulous career in 1930, the "Emperor of Golf" miraculously achieved the feat of winning four major titles in a single year which became renowned as the great "Grand Slam of Golf."

Although Bobby Jones retired from competitive golf after his phenomenal grand slam, his dedicated interest in the game continued. Bobby and some friends purchased a parcel of land and developed a golf course which is now internationally known as the Augusta National Golf Club. The club instituted the annual Masters Tournament which saw its first light in 1934. It was inevitable that the Masters Tournament, linked with the name of Bobby Jones, would be an instant success and it immediately became one of the four most prestigious major championships.

The Masters Tournament, now in its 38th year, is the youngest of the major championships. It is however, without doubt, the very best organized championship in the entire world.

It has been my pleasure to attend 19 consecutive Masters events as a patron and later as a golf scribe. I've seen the numerous progressive improvements which the club has made during this period. Never have I seen a group more dedicated with the intense desire and anxious endeavor to make whatever improvements they can which will benefit the patron (those who pay the cost which most tournaments forget).

From the competitors' point of view, Jack Nicklaus sums it up very well in his letter to Bobby Jones, the President, and Clifford Roberts, the astute Chairman of the Tournament Committee:

As usual, the tournament was run with the dignity and perfection that will never be topped in the game of golf. I want to thank you both very much for allowing me to compete in this tournament. As I have said, Augusta National is my favorite golf course and the Masters my favorite golf tournament. I feel the Masters is a monument to everything great in golf.

Sincerely,
(s) Jack Nicklaus

Bobby Jones himself once related the mission of the Masters Tournament:

The Club's chief objective is to stage a golf show that is enjoyable to all—our members, patrons and player guests, and to interested golfers generally. We would also like, if we can, to contribute something to the advancement of the game.

(s) Robert T. Jones, Jr.
President
Augusta National G.C.

The great Bobby Jones enthralled millions in bygone days with his most incredible performance of play. Now retired to greener fairways, his present and future contribution to the game, unless "we dust thy art to bring returneth" is the Masters Tournament which Jack Nicklaus claims ". . . . is a monument to everything great in golf."

Contents

Publisher's Note *9*

Prologue *11*

Acknowledgments *13*

1 Tommy Aaron *17*
2 George Archer *21*
3 Al Balding *26*
4 Al Besselink *30*
5 Jack Burke, Jr. *33*
6 Billy Casper *36*
7 Bruce Crampton *43*
8 Jimmy D'Angelo *47*
9 Roberto de Vicenzo *50*
10 Charles Evans *54*
11 Jim Ferrier *60*
12 Doug Ford *64*
13 Al Geiberger *69*
14 Nevin H. Gibson *73*
15 Bob Goalby *76*
16 Ralph Guldahl *80*
17 Paul Harney *86*

18 Dave Hill *90*
19 Ben Hogan *95*
20 Tony Jacklin *102*
21 Ruth Jessen *107*
22 Bobby Jones *111*
23 Tony Lema *116*
24 Bob Murphy *119*
25 Jack Nicklaus *123*
26 Arnold Palmer *130*
27 Johnny Pott *135*
28 Dave Ragan *138*
29 Chi Chi Rodriguez *141*
30 Barbara Romack *146*
31 Gene Sarazen *150*
32 Sam Snead *155*
33 Dave Stockton *160*
34 Bob Toski *164*
35 Lee Trevino *167*
36 Ken Venturi *173*
37 Art Wall *181*
38 Lew Worsham *186*
39 Dudley Wysong, Jr. *190*

Publisher's Note

The late Grantland Rice read the manuscript for the *Encyclopedia of Golf* when it was first presented to A. S. Barnes and Company for publication, in 1954. Nevin H. Gibson's material filled two suitcases at that point. "Granny" had been commissioned to compile such a book, but did not have the time. After examining the manuscript, the great sports writer said, "No one but a most dedicated devotee of the game would ever undertake and complete a project as monumental as the one I have just reviewed. This lad has brushed the cobwebs and dusted the records to bring out some of the best facets of the game. It should be published, by all means, as it will be a tremendous contribution to the golfing world."

A few months later Rice died, and eventually the Barnes company changed hands. Other writers submitted golf record books but Gibson's work remained the best and in 1958 it was published. The book is still revised from time to time with up-to-date records and data.

One might think that such a laborious research and writing effort would have satisfied anyone's literary desires but this was not the case. Gibson continued his labor of love and produced *A Pictorial History of Golf*, a colorful array of some 300 photographs, illustrating over 400 years of golfing history.

In between these two classics Major Gibson, having retired from the Air Force, followed the professional golf tour and played in some pro-amateur tournaments. Along the way he met professional Charlie Bassler, and together they produced an instruction book, *You Can Play Par Golf*, now in its third printing.

Some years ago, Nevin Gibson became a member of the Golf Writers Association of America, under the sponsorship of Larry Robinson, then of the *New York World-Telegram*. Introducing the new member the late Charlie Bartlett of the *Chicago Tribune*, the Association's Secretary, said, "Nevin does not write on the surface of this sport. He digs into the depth of the game to explore and reveal subjects which we daily column writers overlook." This statement is borne out once again in *Great Moments in Golf*. In this book the author digs below the surface of bare facts to reveal the emotions felt by great golfers as they experienced their greatest moments in the sport. This is a unique approach to golf writing, and one we are confident will be as enthusiastically received by readers as Gibson's previous books.

Prologue

This book contains those great moments which were experienced by some of the leading golfers of the world. These priceless narrations cannot be measured in terms of monetary values. Such great moments came after many trials and tribulations to those who strived so long and so hard and finally achieved that objective which quenched that seemingly fruitless endeavor, to conquer that stalwart challenge of mind over body.

Acknowledgments

Recording these "great moments" was a labor of love. Seemingly an easy task, the finished product became a reality only through the valuable assistance I received from many supporters. In addition to those leading golfers which are contained herein, who promptly responded to my request for a narrative of their greatest moments, I wish also to express my most sincere appreciation to the following individuals who made valuable contributions to this effort:

Freddy Corcoran, International Golf Association, New York, New York

Desmond ("Des") Sullivan, *Newark* (New Jersey) *News* (Now retired at Myrtle Beach, S.C.)

Donald ("Doc") Giffin, Assistant to Arnold Palmer, Youngstown, Pennsylvania

Robert ("Bob") Sommers, United States Golf Association, New York, New York

Richard ("Dick") Taylor, *Golf World* Magazine, Southern Pines, North Carolina

Oscar Fraley, *Golf* Magazine & Oscar Fraley Associates, Ft. Lauderdale, Florida

Charlie Chamberlain, Associated Press, Chicago, Illinois

Larry Fox, Sports Editor and Writer of "Little Men in Sports"

Will Grimsley, Associated Press, New York, New York

Bud Harvey, *PGA* Magazine, Palm Beach Gardens, Florida

Eugene L. Scott, Sports Investors, Cleveland, Ohio

Bob Rickey, McGregor Company, Cincinnati, Ohio

Eldon Thompson, *Golf World* Magazine, Southern Pines, North Carolina

Edward L. Barner, Uni-Managers International, Los Angeles, California

Eddie Elias, Eddie Elias Enterprises, Akron, Ohio

Leo Fraser, Former President PGA, Atlantic City, New Jersey

Larry A. Blakely, Colonel, USA Ret., with Lee Trevino, Texas

Frank Faulkner, Spalding, Massachusetts

Paul Macdonald, Dunlop Company, Buffalo, New York

Marshall Dann, Western Golf Association, Golf, Illinois

Great Moments in Golf •

William ("Bill") Davis, *Golf Digest*, Norwalk, Connecticut
Bing Crosby, Crosby-Clambake, Beverly Hills, California
Charles L. Foley, International Management, Cleveland, Ohio
Bob Hope, Bob Hope Enterprises, North Hollywood, California
Arline Daley, Secretary, Chicago, Illinois
Ann M. Byrd, Secretary for Jack Nicklaus, Palm Beach, Florida
Terry McVeigh, Secretary for Sports Investors, Cleveland, Ohio
Jean S. Marshall, Secretary to Robert Tyre Jones, Jr.

And to the many others who inadvertently may have been omitted from the above list. My apologies for these omissions.

1
Tommy Aaron

The scattered snow-white clouds, contrasted with the blue Canadian sky, signified a clear day on the 28th day of July, 1969, when Tommy Aaron faced Sam Snead on the first tee of the Pinegrove Golf Course, to vie in that historic playoff for the Canadian Open Championship.

This playoff was most unique in view of the incomparable difference between the two contestants. The soft-spoken, quiet Tommy Aaron who had never won a single pro tournament would match strokes with the venerable 57 year old veteran "Slamming" Sammy Snead who had established a most impressive world record by winning 131 tournaments, including seven major Championship titles.

In no other tournament have the spectators ever pulled for both participants to win. Sam, who had previously won three Canadian Opens, was most popular and many were anxious to see the aging Slammer retain his prestigious status quo to win after 28 years. By the same token, the same rooters, plus the new generation, wanted to see Tommy, who had strived in vain for nine long years to win a single event, become victorious for the first time.

Prior to the play-off, it was the consensus of the large majority that Mr. Snead still retained the necessary credentials to capture his fourth Canadian Open title. Sam's psychological talents to reduce the potential ability of his young golfing opponents from a positive will to a negative approach had been demonstrated over the years. Under these circumstances, it was inconceivable that this would be the championship which marked Tommy Aaron's first victory.

During the championship proper, the great Slammer held the lead during the entire tournament. In the final round, Tommy Aaron scored a most incredible eight under par—64 to tie Sam at 275. When Sam signed his card he turned to an almost shy Aaron and quizzed, "Why'd you pick this day to set a record? What the heck do you think you're doing? Man, I'm tired." Said Tommy, "I didn't even know I'd caught you until the 18th."

The night before the playoff, Tommy Aaron thought of a thousand things. A graduate of the University of Florida in 1960, Tommy had dominated amateur golf in Georgia. He won the Georgia Open three

A close up of Thomas Dean Aaron. The 6′ 1″, 180 pound Georgian possesses one of the smoothest swings in the game. Tommy's first professional victory was the 1969 Canadian Open Championship in which he defeated the master swinger, Samuel Jackson Snead, in an 18 hole play-off. It was Tommy's greatest moment in golf. (Photo by Spalding)

times, the Georgia and Southeastern Amateur twice each and gained national recognition by reaching the finals of the U.S. Amateur Championship and by capturing the 1959 Sunnehanna and the 1960 Western Amateur. He was also a member of the 1959 Walker Cup Team.

These feats, although most impressive in the amateur ranks, could never be compared, even with the greatest imagination, to that most fabulous record established by the immortal, Samual Jackson Snead.

Since joining the professional tour in 1960, Tommy had won over $365,000. Yet he had never won a single tournament. Foremost on Tommy's mind was the fact that he had finished or tied for second *nine times* including two events earlier during the ensuing year. Was this to be the *tenth* time?

The long wait Tommy experienced overnight may be surmised, whereas the Slammer probably had trouble staying awake through the late TV show. To add anguish, Tommy realized that Sam had regained his putting touch after a most profitable lesson from Jerry Barber.

The mental torture which Tommy endured the night before, which perhaps lasted into the wee hours of the day, were now bygone. And once again, he was challenged and the eyes of the golfing world were focused on the outcome.

As it came to pass, the play-off commenced and Tommy Aaron just kept it going like the day before. He took a one shot lead, 34 to 35, after nine holes with a birdie on the ninth. Coming in, he lost two strokes and was down one after 11 holes, but he refused to crack. He got two back at 13 and 14 and with a flourish eagled the 18th as Sam birdied. The long wait was over. Tommy Aaron had won his first tournament by defeating one of the all-time great golfers of the world in a head-to-head battle. He finally conquered the plague which had jinxed him over nine long years.

It was inevitable after this first victory that Tommy Aaron would soon be victorious again. It occurred on the 24th of May, 1970, and most appropriately at a venue in his native state of Georgia. The quiet and soft spoken Georgian won the Atlanta Golf Classic in the presence of those who knew that Thomas Dean Aaron, who had captured every amateur title in Georgia, did indeed possess those qualifications which were necessary to compete and succeed on the professional Tour.

During the decade of the 1960's, Tommy's "Tournament Play Scoring Average" was 71.699 per round. He was in 20th place on the Money Leaders List with earnings of $356,439.15. In 1970, his "Tournament Play Scoring Average was 71.13 and his official earnings totaled $97,980, bringing his all-time earnings to $424,419.15 (through 1970). In 1971 Tommy earned $71,573.25 which increased his career earnings to $509,218.46.

Beyond the snow-white sand of the trap in the fore is the soft velvet grass green. Both can be most hazardous. Here Tommy Aaron barely misses a seemingly easy birdie-putt on the 10th green of the National PGA Golf Course during the 1971 National PGA Championship. Seconds later, Julius Boros, looking on, missed one even shorter. (Photo by Nevin H. Gibson)

Tommy Aaron relates his greatest moment in golf:

Considering the way that I won and the fact that it was my first professional victory, I must say the 1969 Canadian Open is my greatest thrill as a pro. Hopefully, I will have other victories which may overshadow the Canadian Open, but at present, this was a great moment for me.

Shooting a 64 the final round to come from six strokes behind to catch Sam Snead, and then beating him the next day in a play-off should be enough to give anyone a thrill.

1969 was a very rewarding year not only for the Canadian Open but also because I made the Ryder Cup Team.

(s) Tommy Aaron

2
George Archer

George William Archer is one of the many new-comers who joined the professional tour in the 1960's. The tallest professional on the circuit (6'6"), Archer earned $14,867 during his first year on the pro tour in 1964. Since then and during a relatively short period, his name is invariably among the first to be mentioned as he has become one of the top leading money winners among the present crop of youthful professionals. In fact, he is *the* top money winner since the time he joined the PGA tour.

George Archer, very modest and one of the most personable in the ranks of the touring professionals, has earned over $500,000 since he became a professional. By the time this book is printed, this figure may be far from correct at the rate he is going.

George captured his first professional championship, the Lucky International, at a most appropriate venue—in his native city of San Francisco in 1965. In 1966, his best efforts were finishing third in four championships with official earnings of $44,572.42. In 1967, he won the Greensboro Open and in the following year, 1968, he clicked by winning the Pensacola Open, the New Orleans Open and teamed with Bobby Nichols to win the PGA National Team Championship. His official earnings were $150,972.54.

Although plagued with illness for the most part of 1969, he captured the Bing Crosby Invitational and followed this by winning the prestigious title of the Masters Tournament. In spite of his infrequent play during the year, he won $102,702 in official earnings.

In 1970, still with physical ailments, he finished second on two occasions but earned $63,607. During the decade of the 1960's, Bud Harvey of the PGA staff compiled the statistics of the leaders during this period. Although George played only six years of this period according to the records, he ranked among the leaders who had played the entire decade in all categories: the money earned, leading tournament finishers and in the stroke average department.

On January 31, 1971, George scored a string of four birdies from the ninth through the 12th hole and added two more on the final two holes of the Andy Williams–San Diego Open to finish with a sizzling

Big George Archer, referred to as the "Gilroy Cowboy," makes a left-foot spur and a right-hand lash for his birdie effort on the first hole of the Augusta National Golf Course during the 1969 Masters Tournament. He missed his birdie here but the cowboy won the prestigious title which became his greatest moment in golf. (Photo furnished by George Archer)

The smiling George Archer, with every reason to be—the personable "Gilroy cowboy" just won the title of the prestigious Masters Tournament of 1969. (Photo by Wilson)

65 and a 272 total to win the thirty grand prize. In September, he won the Hartford Open after a play-off and his annual winnings of $147,769.10 increased his career earnings to $583,320.44.

Before becoming a professional, George won the Trans-Mississippi Amateur, the San Francisco City Amateur, the Northern California Open and was a semi-finalist in the United States Amateur Championship in 1963.

Referred to as the Gilroy Cowboy, George makes no claim to the title. He responds that cowboys have certain skills which he does not possess, but being the good natured type, he makes no objections to the title he was given. This cowboy bit was derived when the Archer family occupied a house on a ranch which was made available by a close friend. The ranch is located in Gilroy, California.

George Archer is referred to as one of the best putters on the Tour. He proved this point most conclusively at the Glen Campbell Los Angeles Open in 1972 when he made birdies on the final two holes which placed him in a tie. He then, with the magic of his putter, defeated Dave Hill and Tommy Aaron in the 18 hole play-off for his ninth Tour victory.

George Archer relates his greatest moment in golf:

Actually, my first instinct is to say that I haven't had it yet, but that wouldn't really be true. I suppose that the greatest moment I have had in golf was in 1969 when I was ready to hit my second shot to the 18th green at the Augusta National Golf Club.

At that point in the tournament, I had a one stroke lead over three other golfers and I knew that I had to reach the green in good position and I had to make my best effort for a possible birdie. Bill Casper was playing behind me, one stroke behind, and if he birdied any hole, we would be tied. So for sure a birdie would secure the tournament for me. A par might do it, too, but at that point, there was no way to be sure. I did know one thing though, and that was I couldn't play it safe. I had to go for the pin, whether I blew the whole tournament or not. I don't believe that I was too nervous at this time. It was almost over then and I had spent 17 holes being nervous. The winner would be decided very soon. I took out my five iron, oblivious to everything

Big George Archer, 6′ 6″ and the tallest professional on Tour, watches his putt rim the hole on the second green of the Arizona Country Club Course during the 1971 Phoenix Open. One week later, his putts acted better—he won the Andy Williams-San Diego Open. (Photo by Nevin H. Gibson)

going on around me. I studied the shot and stood up to the ball. If I missed the difficult green, the tournament was over for me. I then proceeded to hit one of the finest iron shots I have ever hit in tournament golf under pressure. I don't think, under any circumstances, I could hit a better one. It sailed straight and true, hit the green and bounced a little left, leaving me about an eight to 10 foot putt.

I never have felt the elation I felt at that moment. I believe Arnold Palmer said that this iron shot was one of the best he had ever seen under these circumstances at Augusta. I felt then, before I walked up to the green, that this shot won the Masters for me. I putted, barely missing the insurance birdie, and when Casper failed to birdie this hole, the title indeed belonged to me. This was my "greatest moment in golf." I have been very fortunate in this golf game, and I am very grateful for all it has done for me.

(s)   George Archer

3
Al Balding

Al got his start in golf, as did so many other professionals, as a caddie. He was forced to quit school after the eighth grade to help with family finances. Naturally, as a caddie, Al soon began playing in caddie tournaments. Until after the war, that was his only competition and his only sport.

Balding didn't swing a golf club from 1941 until 1949. After three years' service with the Royal Canadian Artillery during World War II, Al worked three years for a Toronto tire manufacturing company. He happened to win one of the company's employee tournaments and that started him thinking about a career in golf. He quit his job with the tire company because he backed too close to a hot air pipe at home one day and contracted bursitis in the right shoulder as a result of a sudden shoulder movement. This condition still bothers Al occasionally.

While driving transport trucks for a Toronto brewery, Al was asked to become a weekend starter at Oakdale Country Club in Toronto. In 1949, he became assistant professional at that club and had to quit his truck driving job because of a conflict.

"I hope you know what you're doing," said Al's father when he announced his plans to go into professional golf in 1950. The rangy, 6' 2½", 175 pounder knew all right. However, his father didn't live to see his son succeed.

Later Al became assistant at the Burlington Golf Club near Toronto, and in 1951 taught at a Toronto golf school. He won the Canadian Assistants championship in 1951 and the Montreal Open the next year.

At age 35, the native of Mount Dennis, Ontario, was a complete unknown when he became the first Canadian to win a PGA co-sponsored event in the United States, the 1955 Mayfair Inn Open at Sanford, Florida. He defeated Ed Oliver by a stroke. Before winning at Sanford, Al had done pretty well in Canada, but when the slender stylist made his first Winter Tour in 1952 he failed to win a dime in eight starts.

Balding authored one of golf's greatest success stories as he zoomed from 50th on the 1956 money list to eighth in the official PGA cash

The popular Al Balding, the first Canadian professional to win a United States PGA event. The venerable "part-time Tour player" is seen here in Rome, Italy, during the World Cup Championship in 1968 which he won individually, and teamed with fellow-Canadian George Knudson, they won the Cup for Canada. It was Al's greatest moment in golf. (Photo by courtesy of *Golf World Magazine*)

standing in 1957. He won the Miami Beach and the West Palm Beach Opens and established himself as one of golf's top performers. By now, Al was a two-time winner of the Canadian PGA title, ascribing his tremendous improvement in 1957 to experience. Oddly enough, Al's three U.S. victories were scored in the semi-tropical zones in Florida.

After a brilliant 1957, Al tapered off. Then in 1961, "Big Al" engineered one of the PGA Tour's best comebacks, which marked the second time he made successful returns after fading from the lime-lights. In the first nine months, in 27 regulation 72-hole events, he won $17,681.59 in official U.S. PGA earnings. He finished second to Arnold Palmer in the San Diego and Texas Opens and tied for third in the Portland Open. At San Diego, he closed with an incredible "come-from-behind" 66 to tie Palmer, but then he lost in the sudden-death play-off.

Al feels that it is much harder for Canadians to become successful tournament players. "Not only is the season shorter than in most parts of the States," he explains, "but Canadian pros don't get sufficient chance to teach. And teaching is one of the best ways to learn golf."

In 1963, Al won the Mexican Open Championship which gave him titles in three different countries. In addition to Al's four outright United States victories, he was runner-up or tied for second on eight occasions during the period from 1957 through 1964 and he won in excess of $100,000 in official U.S. PGA earnings alone. Al discontinued the regular tour grind in 1964 but played on tour spasmodically.

Although playing infrequently, the popular Canadian professional, representing Canada in the World Cup Championship, teamed with his counterpart George Knudsen, won the World Cup for Canada and Al himself won the individual honors in 1968 at Rome, Italy.

In 1970, the part-time touring professional won his eighth Canadian PGA Championship, which gave him a record of four Canadian PGA Match Play Championships and four Canadian PGA Medal Play Championships.

Al Balding relates his greatest moment in golf:

I have been a golf professional for twenty-one years and was fortunate enough to be the first Canadian to win a United States tour title. The greatest moment in my golfing career came in Rome in 1968.

The tournament was the World Cup Matches and I was teamed with George Knudsen to represent Canada. I had been off the Tour for most of 1967 with a shoulder ailment and played only a smattering of tournaments in 1968. Despite my infrequent play, it seemed that I was like a good wine—getting better with age. And so, appropriately, I chose Italy to achieve my greatest moment.

The tournament was played at the Olgiata Golf Club and teams from 44 Nations were represented. Undoubtedly it was the feeling of playing for your country that made victory to George and I seem so good. But winning the International Trophy for the best individual performance was the icing on the cake.

Becoming the first Canadian to win a United States tour title in 1955 at the Mayfair Inn Open, or the three other tour titles which I have acquired, took a back seat to that week in Rome.

(s) Al Balding

4
Al Besselink

Al Besselink, the 6' 4" blond giant and one of golf's most colorful personalities, became a professional in 1949. His first major victory in the professional ranks came in Iowa where he scored a 266 total to win the Sioux City Open on July 27, 1952. Earlier in the year, Al made an impressive showing in the Masters tournament where he finished third.

In 1953 he won the first Tournament of Champions in Las Vegas and donated half his purse of $10,000 to the Damon Runyan Cancer Fund. This act is most characteristic of Al's nature. Dapper, dashing and debonair, he is a big spender and lives on a high plane. Al would rather be a celebrity than a millionaire. In 1954, Al made a courageous effort in defense of his Tournament of Champions title but Art Wall was victorious with a 278 and Al came in second.

Al won the Havana Invitational Championship in 1956 and in the year following, he won the Kansas City Open and the Caracas Open. In winning the Caracas, he defeated Bob Rosburg in a sudden-death play-off. Just one week later, he lost in a sudden-death play-off against Al Balding to lose the Havana Invitational Championship, the title he was defending.

In 1964 Al won the Azalea Open and in 1965, he captured his second Caracas Open. He was teamed with another colorful professional, Doug Sanders, in the National PGA Team Championship in 1966, but they came in second to the two immortals, Arnold Palmer and Jack Nicklaus who won $25,000 each for their most phenomenal score of 256.

Al, born in Merchantville, New Jersey, before turning professional, was a golf star at the University of Miami and won the Southern Intercollegiate Championship in 1948 and 1949. Al recalls, "I went to Miami with $30 and spent $30,000 there." To those who know Al Besselink, this would come as no surprise.

Al Besselink relates his greatest moment in golf:

I have had many great moments in golf but I cherish this one the most. In playing the final round of the first Tournament of Champions in Las Vegas, Nevada, in 1953, I walked off the 15th green only to

Big Al Besselink recovers from the trap during a tournament in 1950. The 6′ 4″ blond giant scored his greatest moment in golf by winning the first Tournament of Champions event in Las Vegas in 1953. He gave half his winning $10,000 to the Damon Runyon Cancer Fund. (Photo by courtesy of *Golf World Magazine*)

find out that Chandler Harper had just finished his round and I was now one shot behind him with three holes to go, after leading the tournament for the whole four days.

I birdied the par-3 16th hole with a 12-foot putt. On the 17th hole I hit a great seven-iron six feet from the hole and made a beautiful sidehill putt to walk off the green with the gallery cheering wildly. As I teed off the final hole, I knew a par-4 would win the championship. With the big lake on the right of the fairway I aimed far to the left and swung as hard as I could. When I looked up I saw the ball go right down the middle of the fairway. I decided to hit a five-iron and I hit a great shot right at the pin but as I hit it a strong wind came up and the ball hit the green but stopped about three feet off the green. Now I had a forty-foot chip shot right up a hill. I wanted to keep the ball short of the hole and could have an easy up-hill putt. I don't have to tell you where I hit my chip to—ten feet past the hole. Now I was faced with a lightning-fast six-foot breaking down-hill putt. I was all set to roll the ball toward the hole, leaving me with this putt to tie for the tournament and if I missed it I would have finished second.

Now all this was taking place in my mind within 60 to 90 seconds. When all of a sudden it occurred to me that I was going to give half the $10,000 purse to the Walter Winchell-Damon Runyon fund and that the man upstairs would be with me. So at that very moment I decided to take a shot at making the first putt. With the utmost confidence I stroked the ball firmly six feet to the left of the hole and it made a fast break right into the hole, making me the first Tournament of Champions Winner.

(s) Al Besselink

5
Jack Burke, Jr.

There are very few honors which have eluded John Joseph Burke, Jr., better known as Jack Burke. The handsome little Texan (5′ 9″) turned professional in 1941 and served with the U.S. Marine Corps during World War II which postponed his joining the golf tour. He held various club positions until joining the touring professionals in 1950.

Jack immediately proved his professional prowess during his very first year on the Tour. He won the Metropolitan Open, Rio Grande Open, St. Petersburg Open and the Sioux City Open all in the same year.

The next year he won four consecutive tournament victories from the period of February 17th through March 9th. During this year he also won the Vardon Trophy with the lowest scoring average of 70.54.

Becoming one of the tournament's leading stars, his greatest year came in 1956 when he captured the prestigious Masters Tournament title and the National PGA Championship. In winning the Masters, he did the impossible. He trailed Amateur Ken Venturi, the leader, by eight strokes and Cary Middlecoff by six after the third round. In the final round he made up a deficit of eight strokes to edge out Venturi for the victory. Following the Masters, Jack ventured to the Blue Hills Country Club in Canton, Mass., the venue for the National PGA Championship. It was then a most grueling, but exciting, match-play event, with man against man, hole by hole. Jack traveled a very rough route all the way. Fred Haas, Jr., carried him to the 20th hole in the second match and in the semi-finals, Ed Furgol had him five down after 14 holes, but Burke retaliated and finally won on the 37th hole with a birdie. Then in the finals, he was three down after 19 holes to Ted Kroll, but Jack made an incredible string of four consecutive birdies to win by 3 and 2. Burke exhibited one of the greatest match play performances in the history of the tournament.

Jack was a member of five U.S. Ryder Cup teams, 1951, 1953, 1955, 1957 and 1959. He captained the 1957 team to a 7 to 4 victory. A hand injury prevented him from playing in the 1959 matches. Jack had a most impressive record in his Ryder Cup play. He won all four

This solid swing of Jack Burke, Jr., was good enough to earn him two major championships, four consecutive tournament victories and a host of other awards. Jack and his fellow-Texan partner Jimmy Demaret own and operate the fabulous Champions Golf Club in Houston which hosted the Ryder Cup Matches in 1967 and the United States Open in 1969. (Photo by MacGregor)

of his doubles matches and three out of four singles.

By 1963, Jack was spending more time at the Champions Golf Club course, which he and fellow-Texan Jimmy Demaret operate just outside of Houston, than on the Tour. During this year, he made only 16 starts, but won the $50,000 Lucky International at San Francisco and the Texas Open for the second time.

During his playing career, the ex-caddy who worked in his father's golf shop at the River Oaks Country Club in Houston, won $236,360 in official earnings, a figure topped by only 10 other professionals. Jack is limiting his tour appearances considerably, preferring to keep close contact with his famed Houston Champions Golf Club. This most outstanding golf club, which Jack and his partner made famous, was the host to the Ryder Cup Matches in 1967 and the U.S. Open Championships in 1969. This is truly one of the greatest golf clubs of the world. Apart from the two outstanding golf courses, the clubhouse features a most unique concept in design. Every facility, particularly the fabulous and unusual locker rooms, have been planned for convenience and luxurious living.

Jack Burke relates his greatest moments in golf:

As for my "greatest moment" in golf, it would be impossible for me to break it down to one great moment. Each day that I play is my greatest moment—getting into competition is always the greatest moment (if you are playing well). The other days I would like to return to the ping-pong tables.

Helping to build Champions has been a big moment—watching the Ryder Cup and the U.S. Open being played here was a most thrilling experience. Winning my first tournament, The Harlingen Open, and my first major tournament, the Masters, and winning four PGA tournaments in a row—these were all great moments for me.

I met the mother of my five children while playing—I had better say that was my best moment.

(s) Jack Burke

6
Billy Casper

It was mid-June 1959 during the U.S. Open Championship at **Mamaro**-neck, New York, where Billy Casper impressed me as one of **the** most versatile shot-makers in the game. Mother Nature boasted **her** talent and provided a variety of every type of weather. A series of thunderstorms struck on the third day and the final round was postponed to the following day for the first time in Open history and the beautiful "Winged Foot" golf course became a quagmire. The fourth and final round was played on Sunday in chilly, gusty weather. Billy took the lead on the second day with a brilliant 68 during excellent playing conditions and held on to defeat not only the field of competitors, but Mother Nature as well to win the world's most prestigious championship.

To be sure, Billy had won seven tournaments prior to this period. But this Open victory signified that William Earl Casper, Jr., was on his way to become one of the true immortal golfers of the world.

Now, some eleven years later, among other things, Billy has been one of the top ten leading money winners 12 times in the last 13 years, has earned over one million dollars, has won 47 official PGA tournaments, has had his name appear on the Vardon Trophy five times (no pro has won this most respected award more often) and has been a member of the last six Ryder Cup teams.

Billy Casper's 1959 U.S. Open victory on the East Coast in New York was seven years of history when he met Arnold Palmer in the final round of the same championship, some 3000 miles away on the West Coast in San Francisco. When he stood on the tenth tee, he was seven strokes behind Arnie and scarcely in contention. At this precise time, Ben Hogan had just finished the 18th with a most commendable 70 and his gallery immediately joined Arnie's "Army" to watch the great one add further glory to his fame by winning his ninth major championship. It was on the 13th where Billy dropped a long putt to cut the deficit. At the 15th, Palmer bogeyed and Billy birdied. Now, only three strokes back, Billy was now back in contention. The 604-yard 16th proved disastrous for Arnie who struggled for a bogey-6 while Billy sank a 13-foot birdie. The margin was now

A close up of Billy Casper, one of the present day immortal golfers of the world. Billy's phenomenal record includes three major victories, more than one million dollars in official earnings and 47 official PGA Tour victories. His name appears on the Vardon Trophy five times and no pro has won this respected award more often. He has been a member of the last six Ryder Cup teams. One may wonder how a man so devoted to his large family and church can maintain this pace. Yet, this most exciting, versatile and decisive player shows no signs of letting up. (Photo by Ed Barner)

a single stroke. As the record reads, Billy tied Arnold and won the play-off the following day which was one of the most unusual finishes in the Open history.

In the following year, 1967, Billy won the Carlings at Ontario,

Billy Casper hits an approach shot to the 18th green at the Augusta National Golf Course, en route to his victory at the 1970 Masters Tournament. Billy defeated Gene Littler, a fellow-Californian, in a play-off to win his first Masters title for which he had strived 14 years. (Photo by Nevin H. Gibson)

Canada, where the players severely condemned the condition of the Board of Trade course. Then in 69 at Chicago it rained continually during the last two days but Billy captured his third Western Open title over the soggy Midlothian course. Earlier, during the same year, Billy's vie for the Master's title was one shot off pace. His conservative play on the par-5s on the back nine contributed to his loss, it was so alleged. However, Billy was not disappointed. "I am proud to have finished second. It's just another experience."

Billy's experience paid dividends the following year. He birdied both 13 and 15 to tie Gene Littler at 279 then won the play-off for the coveted Master's title which he had sought for 14 years. The Augusta National played most difficult. The course was dry, the fairways shaggy and the greens ultra-fast. It had been a long, cold winter and the growth was not complete. There was also the swirling wind which made club selections more difficult. Again, Billy proved his versatility and played the shots commensurate to the occasion. Casper has long been known for his putting ability, but the truth is he is strong in every department. Five of these events as described were won under abnormal circumstances, and conditions which were my pleasure to see.

Apart from Billy's playing ability, he is one of the most exciting players on the Tour. His club selections and his execution of play are most decisive. It is a known fact that Billy has never been properly appraised. The term "Big Three," which was adopted from the famed British Triumvirate, was conceived premature to Casper's triumphal achievements. No one would ever refute the miraculous records established by Palmer, Nicklaus and Player. Nor would they discredit their tremendous contribution to golf. However, the records do reveal that Billy Casper won more PGA money in the last five years than Palmer or Nicklaus. He also won twice as many tournaments as any other player in the past three years. Since 1966, he has equaled the PGA tour

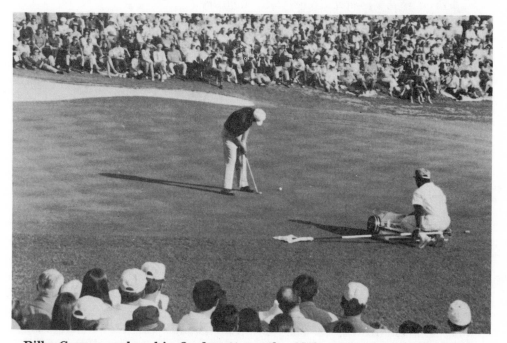

Billy Casper makes his final putt on the 18th green during the 1971 Masters Tournament. Billy was the defending champion, winning the Masters last year after striving to do so for 14 years. (Photo by Nevin H. Gibson)

victories of Palmer, Nicklaus and Player combined. At this rate, Billy will add more records before the ink is dry at this writing.

It would be most difficult to say which of Billy's titles has given him the most satisfaction. When I requested a narrative of his greatest moment in golf, Billy responded with a passage from his great book *My Million Dollar Shots*:

Golf is the greatest game in the world. It is frustrating. It is rewarding. It is humbling. It is humiliating. It is exhilarating. It can send you into the depths of despair. It can rocket you into an orbit of incomparable satisfaction and joy. It teaches. It puts a man's character to the anvil and his richest qualities—patience, poise, restraint—to the flame.

I think I shall never forget June 19, 1966. It was the day I learned the value of restraint.

All sorts of thoughts and temptations were reeling through my head as I teed up the ball on the sixteenth hole in the final round of the U.S. Open Championship at the Olympic Club.

Moments before, I had been a hopelessly beaten man. Paired with Arnold Palmer as the tournament leading twosome, I had fallen seven shots back with only nine holes to play. My only hope at that stage appeared to be to avoid complete disgrace.

Suddenly the match took a dramatic and unbelievable turn. A snakey putt dropped for me on the thirteenth green. At the fifteenth, Palmer bogeyed and I birdied. Now I found myself only three strokes back with three to play. For the first time since Arnold had smothered me with an outgoing 33, I felt I had a chance not just to finish respectably but to win.

Then came the sixteenth, and my honor.

The sixteenth at Olympic is a 604-yard, par five dogleg left that gives the impression of being in another county. My first impulse was that perhaps I should take a jet.

I had a tingling sensation as I teed up the ball. Now I have Palmer reeling, I said to myself, I should now give him the knockout punch. I must not let him regain the initiative.

I looked down the long, narrow canyon and the statuesque trees at the left guarding the shortest approach to the green. "Go for it!" an inner voice counselled. "This is no time to be chicken—let 'er out," urged another voice.

Tension gripped me. Opposite forces battled within me and I could feel them churning. I stepped away from the ball momentarily and took a deep breath. It was just time enough for better judgment to gain control. "Don't change tactics now. Be calm. Play within yourself."

The swing felt good as it went back slowly, reached the desired arc and swept through the ball. It wasn't a tremendously long drive but

Billy Casper drives from the 5th tee at the famed Merion Golf Course during the 1971 U.S. Open Championship at Oakmont, Pennsylvania. This immortal professional won the event on two occasions, 1959 and 1966. Billy has earned over $1,000,000 in official PGA earnings and his name is inscribed on the Vardon Trophy for a record five times. (Photo by Nevin H. Gibson)

it was straight down the fairway. I let out a relieved breath when it came to the end of its roll.

Palmer stepped to the tee. He is strong and bold. For a decade he had thrilled golf fans with his ability to grab a course by the throat and virtually shake it to death. Palmer lashes into the ball with such explosive force that he almost falls off the tee after his follow-through. The word "caution" is not in his vocabulary.

His long lead diminishing and his seemingly certain title now threatened, Arnold felt this was no time for conservatism. With mighty shoulders and arms like those of a blacksmith, he tore into the ball savagely. There was a resounding thunderclap as the club head struck the ball, a wild cheer from the gallery and then a groan. One hundred and eighty yards from the tee, the ball struck a tree and fell limply into Olympic's wiry rough.

Palmer, certainly one of golf's great competitors of all time, was only warming up to the fight. He took a three-iron and waded into the ball. The ball failed to make the fairway. A third shot was necessary to put the ball back into play and a fourth, a desperate wood, sent it flying into a sand trap.

From my fairway position, I was still a long distance from the green. A fairway wood was dictated. Having viewed Arnie's troubles, I decided this was no time to be a hero. I pulled a two-iron from the bag and hit my second shot down the fairway, leaving me still a middle iron to the green. I could have gained greater distance with a wood but I might have discovered greater trouble.

With a five-iron, I pitched my third shot to the green, thirteen feet from the cup. I sank the putt for a birdie. Arnie got down in two from the bunker for a bogey six. His lead was cut to a single stroke.

It is rather common knowledge among followers of the game what happened after that. Arnold and I tied for the title with 278. In the eighteen-hole playoff the next day, Arnie again shot a 33 on the front nine for a two-stroke lead. But the match suddenly reversed itself—as the day before—and I finished with a 69 while Palmer shot 73. This was my greatest moment in golf.

(s) Billy Casper

7
Bruce Crampton

At the youthful age of 20, Bruce Crampton achieved one of his great ambitions when he captured the Australian Open Golf Championship in 1956 to win his country's most highly coveted golf award. However, the words of the press cast a dark shadow over his great victory. Peter Thomson, who reigned supreme during this period, was in Great Britain and did not compete in this Open. Therefore, the big question: could Bruce have won if "Peter The Great" was participating? This publicity obviously dimmed the shining glow of Crampton's incredible victory.

It was inevitable that Bruce and Peter would compete in many future events. It so happened that a fortnight later the Speedo Golf Tournament was scheduled at the Victoria Golf Club in Melbourne and the renowned Peter Thomson would be in contention thereat. This presented a great challenge to Bruce and it was only natural that the press would select the internationally famous Peter Thomson as the big favorite to win. Furthermore, added the press, it was Peter's own venue and he knew every blade of grass thereon.

As Ripley said, "Believe It or Not. . . ." The records show that Bruce Crampton was victorious against all odds. The story of this victory is best told by Bruce himself and related in his "greatest moment in golf" which follows later.

Following his Australian Open victory in 1956, Bruce joined the Tour in the United States early in 1957. He fought very hard and struggled for five years before he reaped his first significant harvest. In 1961, he won the Milwaukee Open which was his first U.S. victory. He captured the Motor City Open in 1962, the Texas Open in 1964 and in 1965 he won three: the Bing Crosby Invitational, the Colonial National and the "500" Festival. After a slump in 1967 and 1968, Bruce bounced back strong in 1968 when he won the West End Classic in the Bahamas and ended the year with official earnings of over $101,000 which placed him 13th on the leading winners' list.

Bruce hit harder in the following year when the Australian, by then Americanized, won the Hawaiian Open with a four-stroke margin over second-placed Jack Nicklaus and by the end of the year he was the fifth

Bruce Crampton drives from the 10th tee of the Westchester Country Club, New York, the site of the Westchester Classic, en route to winning $50,000, the richest event of the year. The week prior, Bruce tied for second and in the event following the Westchester, he was also tied for second, thus winning $69,766.66 in 17 days of play. (Photo by Nevin H. Gibson)

leading money winner with earnings of $118,958.

It was Sunday, August 2, 1970 at the Westchester Golf Classic in Harrison, New York, where Bruce Crampton won his largest purse. He holed out from off the green on two consecutive holes, 16 and 17, then made a legitimate birdie on the 18th for 67 and finished with a 273 total. This gave the curly-haired 34-year old veteran a one stroke lead over Jack Nicklaus and young Larry Hinson, both of whom made sensational eagles on the final hole. This victory was worth $50,000 and brought the converted Texan, now living in Dallas, career earnings to $538,862 and became the second foreign player in history to pass the $500,000 mark. Not bad for the youthful Aussie who commenced at the age of 21.

Through 1965, Bruce Crampton's greatest victory, prestige-wise, in the U.S. was the Colonial National Championship, considered as a semi-major in *The Encyclopedia of Golf*, which he won with birdies on four of the last six holes. Then in 1971 he added another semi-major by winning the Western Open and by the end of the year his earnings of $106,736.26 increased his career earnings to $680,432.63, placing him as the eighth all-time leading money winner. Bruce relates the following as his greatest moment in golf:

First, my biggest thrill was winning the Australian Open which is the National Open in my country. Within the frame of this victory I experienced my "greatest moment in golf" which actually came with the results of a single golf shot which assured my victory. Also, this title gave me an invitation to the Masters Tournament in the U.S., and most fortunately, I have played every year thereat, except one, since my 1956 victory. It also gave me the necessary impetus and confidence to compete with the best golfers in the U.S.

In winning the Australian Open Championship, I led for the first two rounds and was two strokes in front of Kel Nagle. At that time we played 36 holes on the last day.

In the final round, I got to the 11th and was even with Kel. On the 15th and 16th, two back-to-back par-fives, I had a chance on each for a birdie. However, I missed the 15th and when I missed again at the 16th, I felt the world had tumbled on me, as I thought at this point I had thrown the victory away. I was now even with two holes to play. I needed two pars to tie and one birdie and one par to win which at the time seemed impossible in view of my efforts at the 15th and 16th.

After composing myself to some extent, I hit a 3-wood from the tee of the 17th 230-yard par-3 hole on the right front of the green . . . a great shot . . . but some distance from the hole . . . fortunately . . . I dropped the putt for a birdie-2.

The 18th hole was a rather tricky par-4 dogleg to the left. I decided to use the 3-wood again from the tee which left me approximately 160 yards from the green. This upcoming approach shot was the most crucial shot of the tournament. Should I go for it boldly to win, or should I play it safe . . . to tie . . . or possibly lose, I asked myself. I selected a six-iron and let it go all the way . . . it felt perfect . . . it was one of the most beautiful shots I ever made . . . the ball went like a bullet . . . straight to the flag . . . all the way . . . then stopped within four feet of the hole . . . it was my "greatest moment in golf" . . . I knew right then I had won the Championship . . . I knocked the putt in for a birdie 3 to win the Australian Open. This was my greatest thrill and I produced my best when it was required.

To say that my thrill ended there would be incomplete in view of the circumstances which were to follow. It so happened that the press mentioned the fact that Peter Thomson was in Great Britain and did not compete. If there, he would have probably won. It was only a short period of two weeks later when I competed with Peter in the Speedo 90-Hole Golf Tournament at Melbourne over his own Victoria Golf Course. To be sure, this tournament was in no comparison with the prestigious Australian Open Championship. But it came at a time which made it very important to me individually.

After three rounds of play, I held my own and was tied with Peter. This just happened to be on my 21st birthday and the following day we were to play 36 holes to complete the 90-Hole Tournament.

After the morning round Peter had a 70 while I was even par, three strokes back at 73.

During the interlude prior to teeing off in the final round, the press room buzzed the hum that Peter Thomson was back and the complexion of things to come would be different. . . . Peter had just won his third consecutive British Open Championship by three strokes . . . and his three under for the morning round . . . signified that he was now ready to tear the course to pieces. This of course, I just imagined was the pulse of the press. I did however realize that Peter's victory would certainly diminish my credit of winning the Australian Open Championship. Naturally, I thought of many other things at this stage of the tournament. Did I really have it?

Without a chronicle hole-by-hole account, I played my best against ole-man-par, the most formidable foe at all times. I gave him the thrashing of his life when I scored an eight under par for a course record of 65 and to win by four strokes.

Telephoned from Dallas to Chicago by
Bruce Crampton

8
Jimmy D'Angelo

At the youthful age of 21, Jimmy D'Angelo was appointed Club Professional at the Baederwood Golf Club in Jenkintown, Pennsylvania, in 1931 and was the youngest professional in the United States to hold a head professional club position.

Jimmy, one of the game's better teachers, was the first professional to give a golf lesson on television. This program, sponsored by Hale America, a nation-wide physical fitness program designed to keep people participating in sports and keeping fit during the war, took place in March 1942 over Station WPTZ, Chicago, the Philco Station and the pioneers in television.

In May, 1948, Jimmy came to Myrtle Beach, South Carolina, and sold stock in the Dunes Golf Club where he was to become the professional before the course was open for play. He also operated a golf driving range. There was an old golf course at the Beach during the time which was laid out in the early 1900's by Donald Ross but it was outmoded and not conducive for attracting golfers. A tract of property known as the Myrtle Beach Farms Co., in which James Bryan was Secretary and his brother, Buster, was a stock holder, became available for the Dunes Club and these brothers were the prime organizers of the Dunes Golf Club.

Mr. Robert Trent Jones, the famed golf architect, laid out a challenging championship course. The Dunes Golf Club grew rapidly, due in part to the rugged course which became known as one of the most challenging courses and which attracted many of the better golfers.

Early in the 1950's, Larry Robinson, a golf writer then with the New York *World Telegram,* visited his old friend Jimmy, a native of Philadelphia, and suggested honoring Robert Trent Jones with a golf tournament and dinner. Larry contacted Bob Harlow of *Golf World* Magazine and the tournament, which was held in 1954, attracted 8 golf writers and Bob Harlow became the first winner. From this came the Golf Writers Championship. The tournament, which is held one week before the Masters every year, has been a permanent fixture ever since.

The names Jimmy D'Angelo and the Dunes Golf Club are synony-

Jimmy D'Angelo, left, with the author in the Dunes Golf Clubhouse at Myrtle Beach, South Carolina, during the Golf Writers Championship in 1970. Jimmy was the pioneer professional at the Dunes club and was instrumental in making it famous. (Photo by Johnny Olsen)

mous. The Dunes Golf Club, under the professional leadership of Jimmy from the very beginning, was instrumental in bringing golf to the Beach and Myrtle Beach became the first "Golf and Beach Mecca" of the South.

In 1968, Jimmy retired as the Club's professional after twenty years of service. Still living near the premises and in the shadow of the now famous Dunes Golf Clubhouse, he is the Director of Golf for Golf Holiday, an organization comprising twenty motels and ten golf courses in Myrtle Beach.

As one of the great contributors to the game which has risen to such astronomical heights, Jimmy can now relax and from his cozy home, overlooking the beautiful panoramic view which he changed from a wasted dune, reminisce his many experiences. It was on such an occasion when I asked Mr. Jimmy D'Angelo his greatest moment in golf. I was prepared to write a story of one of his many challenging exploits and how he conquered the obstacles to achieve his mission. But Jimmy goes back and quotes an episode which occurred during his early career while in the ranks of a professional golfer:

My greatest moment in golf occurred while playing in the Annual Pro-Amateur Championship of Philadelphia at the Philmont Country Club. Our match throughout the championship was nip and tuck and when we completed the final hole, we were even, which required a sudden-death play-off. On the fifth extra hole, I faded my tee shot to the wiry rough. By the time we approached my ball, my partner was out of contention and the burden rested with me. I was behind a tree and 200 yards from the green. Our opponents were in excellent position and it seemed certain that we were doomed. I surveyed my impossible position. I had to hit a low slice from a tight lie in order to get anywhere near the green. If I could produce such a shot, I could conceivably pitch up close enough for a possible four which may save the hole, but this seemed most improbable. Finally, I selected a three wood and produced my greatest shot in golf. It was a 100 to 1 shot which came off perfect. The ball was low enough to miss the tree's limb, yet it rose high enough for the required slice and it hit the green then stopped within 20 inches of the hole. It was indeed a great thrill to experience this most amazing shot. Our competition pared the hole and I dropped my birdie putt for the final victory. It was not only my greatest shot in golf but it came at the right time and became my "Greatest Moment in Golf."

(s) Jimmy D'Angelo

9
Roberto de Vicenzo

The trees in the rays of the setting sun cast long shadows across the lush fairways of the Augusta National Golf Course and the fresh spring air began to chill on that 14th day of April, 1968.

Enjoying this panoramic view and the thrilling climax of this 31st Annual Masters Tournament were some 25,000 spectators. Within this circular human boundary which surrounded the (Holly) 18th hole walked four lonely figures, two contestants and two caddies who were too intense to appreciate the beauty of this most picturesque scene.

Apart from this throng of thousands were the millions of television fans in the United States and those abroad who were watching via the orbiting satellite.

The center of attraction was focussed on one in the party of four, Roberto de Vicenzo, the world famous international golfer from Buenos Aires and the reigning champion of the British Open Championship.

Roberto, a most popular personality, had won 129 golf tournaments which included 30 Open titles in 14 different countries. He had spread golf's gospel around the world for 25 years and his affection for people and the game was most prominently known throughout the world. He was now par-in for a brilliant 65 and on the verge of winning this most prestigious title. Although he had won nine PGA tour titles, including the Colonial National, he had never captured a major title in the United States. As Roberto approached the green, he received a standing ovation from the gallery who were most anxious to see him win and don the traditional green blazer during the colorful presentation ceremony.

The sound of the excited throng had silenced to the quietness of night and Roberto stroked the final putt for his miraculous 65 and for the apparent winning 277 total score. No less than 20 million people witnessed this most dramatic finish which cinched the victory, or at worst, a tie for the lead. It was Roberto's greatest moment in golf.

After the cheers and within minutes the excited thousands became silent again. This time—for another reason—something was wrong. Then it was true—the dreadful rumor became a reality. Roberto signed an incorrect scorecard which cost him a chance to win in a play-off for the title.

Roberto de Vicenzo, the world famous international professional, is on the practice green of the famed Augusta National Golf Course during the Masters Tournament. It was here in 1968 when Roberto, then the reigning British Open Champion, received his greatest moment in golf —and within minutes, it became his most tragic. From all indications, Roberto had won the Masters title, but a technically incorrect score card prevented the opportunity to vie in a play-off for the title. This most personable and popular world-wide professional accepted the penalty like the true champion he is, without blaming anyone but himself. (Photo by Nevin H. Gibson)

It was ironic that this great moment in golf would revert within minutes to Roberto's most tragic moment in golf. The saddened 45-year-old professional refused to blame anyone but himself. He accepted the decision like a champion, then coined the phrase, "What a stupid I am."

In 1970, the 18th World Cup Championship was played in Buenos Aires in dedication to Roberto. He had played in the first event in 1953 and was on the Argentine Winning team. Not only did he play in the 1970 event but he won the International (Individual) Trophy with a record score of 269.

Roberto won a grand slam of awards in 1970—the Bob Jones award given by the United States Golf Association for sportsmanship, the William D. Richardson Award by the Golf Writers Association of America for his contribution to golf, and he was also honored as the Golfer of the Year at the dinner for the American Cancer Society and given an award for true greatness and sportsmanship. Finally, the World Cup was dedicated to Roberto by the International Golf Association for contributing the most to international golf.

In 1971 the Panama Open was dedicated to Roberto and he won the title with a sparkling 63 on his final round for a 273 total.

Roberto relates his greatest moment in golf:

It was 21 years ago in 1948 when I entered the British Open at Muirfield and one bad round cost me the championship and I ended in a tie for third place. The following year at Sandwich, another bad round placed me in the same position. Then the next year at Troon, I finally played four good rounds, but Bobby Locke's final 68 against my 70 made me the runner-up. After these three consecutive years, when I came so close, it appeared that I was not destined to win this great championship.

When Ben Hogan won at Carnoustie in 1953 by four strokes his closing 68 picked up five strokes on my 73 and I was six strokes off. Following this, I ended in third place on four more occasions during the years of 1956, 1960, 1964 and 1965. I've never really played bad in the British Open, apart from having one bad round, but that's all it takes to lose any championship.

I had competed against two generations which commenced with Henry Cotton and Bobby Locke, then Peter Thomson had his reign, now it was the youthful triumvirate of Player, Palmer and Nicklaus. Time was marching on. I was not immune from growing old and this obviously bothered me.

Then in 1967 at Hoylake—something happened. After two rounds I was one stroke back of Jack Nicklaus, the defending champion, and Bruce Devlin. Then in round three I scored a 67, the same as Gary Player, which were the lowest rounds during the tournament. This gave me a two stroke lead going into the final round.

I thought of last year, when I blew to a 77 in the last round at Muirfield, which was my worst effort in the British Open. I was determined that this wouldn't happen again. A two stroke lead means nothing. Sometimes you are better off, psychologically, to be two strokes back. With Gary Player and "Big" Jack Nicklaus right behind me, I knew I must play and play well to win.

I retained that positive attitude and played well in spite of "Big Jack," who was really making the best effort of the entire field and he showed no signs of letting up.

When I arrived at the 18th tee, I knew then that my previous efforts, which were numerous, in the British Open were not in vain. I was really going to win this great championship in which I had strived so long and so hard. That long walk to the 18th green, with thousands of well wishers cheering and the millions watching on television, was a great thrill and it was indeed my greatest moment in golf.

My second great moment in golf would be at the Jockey Club in my native Buenos Aires in 1962. I finished the World Cup matches to win the individual championship over Arnold Palmer and Sam Snead.

One of my greatest thrills in golf was at the Congressional Country Club in Washington, D.C., when I defeated Sam Snead in the match sponsored by the "Shell's Wonderful World of Golf" in 1967.

I was also most elated to receive the Richardson Award in 1970, when the Golf Writers Association of America voted in my favor as the outstanding contributor to golf for the year.

In summation, golf has been very good to me all over the world and I hope to contribute more to the game. But I shall always remember when I finally won the British Open Championship which was my greatest moment in golf.

(s) Roberto de Vicenzo

10
Charles Evans

With seven hickory-shafted golf clubs, Chick Evans wins the 1916 "Double," from which derived his "greatest moment in golf." This great story is best told by Robert Sommers and is quoted in part from the June 1966 issue of *The Golf Journal*:

The year was 1916. The British Fleet would win at Jutland . . . the land war in Europe would settle into gory stagnation . . . Rasputin would be assassinated in Leningrad . . . Pancho Villa would come North of the border to raid New Mexico. Skirts were long, collars high, hat brims wide. Brooklyn would win glory with its first National League pennant. . . . Tris Speaker would interrupt Ty Cobb's rule by winning the American League batting championship. . . . Elmer Oliphant would lead Army to an undefeated, 9–0 football season. And there was golf and Chick Evans.

Three years before, Francis Ouimet strolled across the street from his Brookline, Mass., home and put golf on the front page by winning the United States Open Championship, beating two men who could not be beaten—Harry Vardon and Ted Ray.

Evans would keep it on the front page, for he would do something that Ouimet could not. Ouimet could not win the Amateur that year when he won the Open; he waited until 1914.

Evans would give America its first "slam" by taking both the Open and the Amateur. John Ball had won the British Amateur and Open in 1890, but so far double victory had escaped American amateurs at home. It would not escape Evans.

Since Evans' memorable double in 1916, it has been done by only one other American. Bob Jones in 1930 with his four-way "Grand Slam" spanning two continents.

But in 1916 the "Grand Slam" was barely thought of. Let an amateur win just two National championships in one year before horizons are expended. Then the break came.

In 1916 the Open moved west, to Minikahda in Minneapolis, the farthest west it had ever gone since its beginning in 1895. There to meet it was Charles Evans, Jr., a dapper young Chicagoan from the Edgewater Club with seven clubs in his bag—brassie, spoon, midiron, jigger, lofter, niblick and putter. Evans in 1916 was far from unknown. Then 26, he had reached the semi-finals of the Amateur four times and lost to Jerry Travers in the 1912 final. He was a perpetual, inconsolable near-miss.

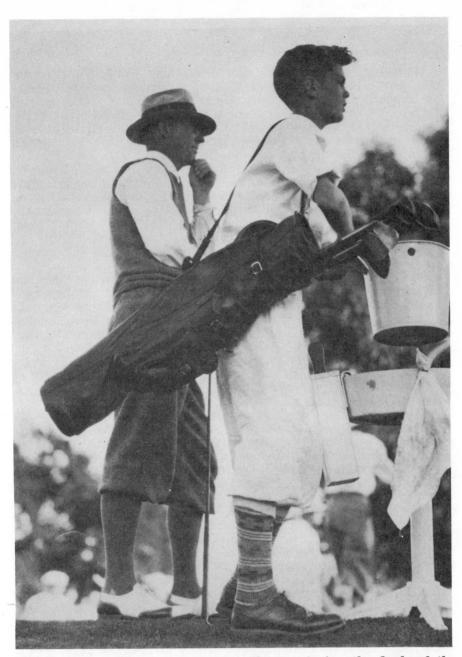

"Chick" Evans thinks a moment on the tee during the finals of the U.S. Amateur in 1927 at Minneapolis. This immortal amateur won both the U.S. Open and the U.S. Amateur Championships in 1916 with the use of seven hickory-shafted clubs and repeated his Amateur victory in 1920. He practically dominated the Western Amateur Championship by winning it for a record of eight times. His name shall forever be boldly emblazoned on the pages of golfing lore. Note Chick's clubs—the same seven he used in 1916. The clean-cut, intense caddy, also wearing plus-fours, is synonymous with Evans. He started the Evans Scholars Foundation which provides college scholarships to deserving young men in which the sponsorship is now assumed by the Western Golf Association. (Photo by D. Scott Chisholm)

He had come within one stroke of matching Walter Hagen's winning 290 in the 1914 Open at Midlothian, picking up seven strokes on Hagen in the final 36 holes. He closed with 71–70—141 against Hagen's 75–73. On the home hole Evans needed an eagle two to tie. He almost did it—his approach stopped nine inches from the hole.

He was known as a fine player, perhaps the best from tee to green in America. He hit crisp, accurate irons.

He was also known as a somewhat ghastly putter under pressure.

With the 1916 Open played so far from the Eastern population centers, the entry list showed a dip. At Baltusrol the year before, 130 players started; at Minikahda, only 81. Among them were names that would become indelible: Hagen, Jock Hutchison, Wilfrid Reid, Jim Barnes, Fred McLeod.

But two of the biggest names, Ouimet and Jerome D. Travers, were missing.

The Open was preceded by a professional-amateur event, and right away Evans showed that, after his years of frustration, perhaps he was ready to win a National Championship. He teamed with Jimmie Donaldson of Chicago to shoot 67–70—137. They thought they had won until late in the day when Reid and Laurence Carpenter came in with 70–67—137 to tie.

The next day was the first day of Open Championship qualifying— 36 holes at the site. Evans didn't play that day. Alec Campbell, of Baltimore, led with 71–73—144. Evans qualified the second day, shooting 75–70—145, one stroke off the lead.

Then began the Championship proper, 72 holes in two days. A heavy rainstorm struck during the night, improving the playing conditions of Minikahda. The turf had been very hard, making control of shots difficult. Now the ball would stay where it was played.

Wilfrid Reid and Evans played the best golf through the morning round. Evans shot 32 on the outgoing nine and found himself only one stroke in the lead; Reid had done 33. Both cooled off coming back with Evans shooting 38 and Reid 37, giving each 70.

In the afternoon Reid forged ahead, playing the outgoing nine in 33 against the 36 of Evans. Reid made a bird two on the 10th but later faltered, finishing with 72.

Evans, meanwhile, came back in 33 and had 69 for the second round, 139 for 36 holes. He was the halfway leader.

Next morning the gray clouds of the day before had disappeared and the weather became hot. A wind rose, affecting drives, and Evans played a steady 74.

For a while this didn't appear good enough, for Reid was still playing masterfully. He made the nine-hole turn in 32 and regained the lead.

Reid, now 81, remembers this version of that fateful round: "I had picked up six strokes on Evans and was in the lead. Then came the catastrophe. With old George Turnbull, of Midlothian, I had to wait 30-odd minutes before playing the 12th. The crowd was now so dense! Most of Hagen's gallery and Chick Evans' big gallery had all swamped into mine. I had only four Boy Scouts as marshals! The 12th was a long, tough, double dog-leg hole with trees on the left, a large hill to carry over and bad trouble on the right. Finally, I drove to the right center, struck someone on the head, and from there on took 7–7–7 and a 47 back for 32–47—79."

Reid was now out of it, but as the fourth round progressed, new threats developed. Few men in America could play as well as Jock Hutchison. His opening 148 left him well behind Evans and Reid, yet he recovered to shoot 72 in the morning and then 68 in the final round—a total of 288. A bit too much.

Jim Barnes after 36 holes had 144, five strokes behind Evans. He shot 71 in the morning round of the final day and picked up three shots. Henry Mackall, of Minneapolis, was in charge of the Evans galleries that final day and remembers what could have been the deciding hole of the Championship.

"At the end of the third round Chick and Jim Barnes were leading. As the last round on Saturday afternoon began, Barnes was playing ahead of Chick. When we got around to the 13th hole, word came back that Barnes had finished with 289."

"The 13th was the longest hole at Minikahda, 525 yards with a creek running through it about 100 yards short of the green. The average player played his second shot short of the creek, then approached onto the green. After hearing Barnes' score, Chick turned to me and said: 'I think I can afford to take a chance.' "

"He took out a brassie and put the ball over the creek onto the green. This gave him a birdie 4, which was sufficient to let him come up the winner."

Evans faltered finally on the home hole, taking three putts. But

Mr. Robert Sommers, Public Information Manager of the U.S. Golf Association, provided the Chick Evans article. (Photo by Nevin H. Gibson)

he had shot 73 in that final round, giving him 286 for the 72 holes and an Open record that would stand unequalled for 16 years and unbroken for 20.

Now on to Philadelphia for the Amateur went Evans and his seven clubs. (Actually, Chick had more than seven clubs for he sometimes carried four putters, so erratic was he on the greens.)

His Open victory seemed to give him added confidence, yet he was not the overwhelming choice. The magazine *Golf* for August, 1916, was extremely tentative in endorsing Chick: "The Open Champion cannot but be a great favorite, but it must be remembered that he has been so near winning so many times that one must always look for a slip-up in his game. . . . He will still be Open Champion, whether he is beaten or not, and that ought to eliminate the nervousness that he has been suffering from on other occasions. There are authorities on the game that insist that if Evans putts as well at Merion as he did at Minikahda he will be the Amateur Champion as well as the Open Champion for 1916. There can be no doubt about his superior ability on all other kinds of play."

This was to be a fateful tournament. It was the introduction of the Merion Cricket Club to a national Championship for men, though twice before it was host to the Women's Amateur. It would see the debut of Bob Jones in National competition. Jones was then 14 and had recently won the Georgia State Championship.

Merion was the only club in America with two courses—the East and the West. Both were to be used for the qualifying rounds; the Championship proper would be played on the East course.

The starting field of 157 was the largest since the Championship was restricted to golfers on the National Eligibility list. Robert A. Gardner, of Chicago, was the defending Champion. He had not been playing steadily and he had a history of frustration on Eastern courses. Grantland Rice remarked:

"Gardner will not be the leading favorite. He has yet to show that he has conquered the Eastern course architecture and mastered the more bewildering Eastern greens."

In the qualifying, Evans shot a comfortable 158, five strokes behind the medalist W. C. Fownes, Jr., of Oakmont. Chick then raced through the first three rounds, beating Nelson M. Whitney, of New Orleans, 3 and 2; W. P. Smith, of Philadelphia, 10 and 9; and John G. Anderson, of New York, 9 and 8.

From the first hole of his match with Whitney it was apparent that Evans' putting was still effective. Whitney put his approach on the green; Evans hooked into a greenside bunker. When he attempted to recover, he sailed his ball well over the green. But Chick pitched back on, about 25 yards from the hole, and made his putt for the half.

In the fourth round he met D. Clarke (Ducky) Corkran, who came up from Baltimore with a good reputation. Again Evans' short game held up, while Corkran's did not and he succumbed, 3 and 2.

Meanwhile, Bob Gardner as defending Champion had mastered Eastern architecture enough to breeze through four matches. He defeated John Ward, of Garden City, New York, Max Marston, of Springfield, New Jersey, and this brought him up against the 14-year-old Bob Jones in the quarter finals. Gardner won, 5 and 3, but it was known by then that Jones would be back. The impressions Jones left are still vivid with Evans:

"I remember the sensational play by which Bobby Jones introduced himself to the golfing world. In one match he won four straight holes from Frank Dyer, drove 280 yards on one hole, put a cleek shot 190 yards over the quarry on the 16th hole to within a foot of the hole, showed nerve under trying conditions and good judgment in selecting clubs in a hair-raising contest."

Safely by Jones, Gardner beat Jesse Guilford, the "human siege gun," 4 and 3.

Now the final—a match which brought together the Open and the Amateur Champions for the first and still the only time in the final. A tremendous gallery was there. Evans went ahead on the first hole, after nine was two up, with 39 out against Gardner's 43, and increased his edge to 3 up at the end of the morning round.

Gardner began to chip away at Evans' lead in the afternoon. At the end of nine holes he was only 1 down and seemed ready to pull even on the 10th when Evans bunkered to the left. Evans came out 25 yards from the hole and holed the putt for a half.

From then on Evans merely added cushion. He won the 12th and 13th to go 3 up, and when he won the 15th the match was over.

One man had won both the Open and the Amateur Championships of the United States!

Evans recalls: "I swung into the last holes carefully, taking no chances. The crowd that swept the course swarmed everywhere after the final putt. The applause echoed and someone pushed my mother forward. She looked very little in that immense crowd. Under her glasses tears of joy glistened, as I, half crying, half laughing, hugged and kissed her. It was a wonderful feeling—the happiest of my life. Winning the double crown made me feel that I was rewarded for all the many hours I had spent mastering golf shots."

11
Jim Ferrier

It was 25 years ago when I first saw "Big" Jim Ferrier at the Tacoma Open Championship of 1945 at the Fircrest Golf Club when the total prize was $10,000 and the winner's share was two grand. I was most anxious to see this huge 6' 3½", long-hitting Aussie in action. However, after the very first hole, I lost all interest. Jim, then a Staff Sergeant on leave from the U.S. Army, started out on this long five-par hole, all up-hill with O.B. on the left of this narrow fairway and his second shot was measured to be "one inch" O.B. Then his next shot, #4 was also O.B. His #6 shot was unplayable for (stroke and distance) and #8 was short of the green from where he pitched on and dropped his putt for a 10. (Actually a birdie-4, plus penalties). After this start I figured he was definitely out of contention.

I departed to watch Charlie Congdon, my own local professional, who was paired with Lord Byron Nelson. Charlie had just sunk a 95-foot putt on the large, undulated fifth green for an eagle-3 and the terrific roar of the partisan spectators can be imagined. Even the icy veins of Lord Byron had temporarily thawed.

Later, there were other roars, shouts and screams coming from the fans following the contestant who was completely out of the contention. Yes, it was Big Jim Ferrier who was making birdie after birdie, striving to overcome his first hole deficit. Big Jim's efforts were not in vain. When he finished the 18th hole, his score card read 73. At the end of the tournament, Jim was tied for third place which was indeed a most magnificent effort considering the fat 10 he took on the very first hole. Few golfers possess such fortitude to play so brilliantly following such a most disastrous beginning. During this same year, Jim won the San Francisco Open (after scoring two-holes-in-one) and the Northern California Open for the second time.

Born in Sydney, Australia, Jim won practically every amateur tournament "down-under" before coming to the United States to turn professional in 1940. His first victory was the State Championship in Sydney at the age of 16 in 1931. Thirty years later in 1961 at the age of 46, he won the Almaden Open Championship. In between this thirty year span, and excluding his foreign record, Jim has won 22 tourna-

Big Jim Ferrier, a 6' 3½" Aussie, is seen here in close contention for the U.S. Open Championship title at the Merion Country Club, Oakmont, Pennsylvania, in 1950. His 289 score was two strokes off Ben Hogan's winning pace of 287. Jim's greatest moment in golf came during his National PGA Championship victory in 1947 at Detroit. (Photo by courtesy of *Golf World Magazine*)

ments and his career is highlighted with the following feats:

Four-time winner, Australian Amateur, 1935, 1936, 1938 and 1939.

Twice winner, Australian Open, 1938 and 1939.

Winner, National P.G.A. (match play) Championship, 1947.

Twice winner, Canadian Open Championship, 1950 and 1951.

Second Leading Money Winner, 1950.

Runner-up, Masters Tournament, 1950.

Runner-up, National P.G.A. (stroke-play) Championship, 1960.

Although Jim's last big victory came in 1961, he frequently plays in the major events, which is some pace for the venerable 55-year veteran. In 1964, he was tied for fifth place in the Masters Tournament and for sixth place in the Western Open. In August 1970, Jim finished with a 288 total in the Dow Jones Open on the Upper Montclair course in Clifton, New Jersey, after an opening round of 68, to win $1211.

What led up to become Jim's great moment in golf was actually a single golf shot. This occurred on the 21st hole of the 1947 P.G.A. Championship and Jim quotes from his book *Low Score Golf* the following account:

The twenty-first or third hole at Plum Hollow is 442 yards in length. To the right of the fairway is an out-of-bounds fence flanked with shrubs. I was a little bit quick on my drive, pushing it to the right and apparently the ball went into the bushes just inside the fence. Chick's drive was a beauty, 300 yards down the middle.

We found my ball lying on a tarpaulin which had been hung between two bushes. This was right along a golf equipment shed. The ball was at least a foot off the ground. Byron Nelson was refereeing the match and he ruled that the ball could be lifted, the canvas removed, and the ball dropped exactly where it had come to rest, without penalty.

This was done, but I was now in a tight spot. My ball was lying so close to the bushes that I couldn't swing toward the green. I could take a putter and hit back into the fairway but that would actually mean giving the hole to Harbert.

A rather strong wind was blowing, coming in a bit from the left and into my face. If I could play a wide hook, out of bounds, it might be possible to take advantage of the head-wind and get somewhere near the green. It was a do-or-die chance and I decided to risk it.

I took a number five iron, stood for a wide hook, and hit hard. It had to be a crisply hit shot to get anywhere against the wind. That ball traveled as if it had eyes. It got up fast, cleared the trees, sailed out over the barn and then came in toward the green. As it met the full force of the headwind the ball dropped almost straight, right onto the green and almost dead to the pin.

Chick was flabbergasted. Nelson said it was such a shot as he had never seen and never again expected to see. From that minute on I knew that I was going to win. I dropped the putt for a birdie and won the hole. To be sure I lost the next with a bogey, but I came back with a birdie "2" at the following hole, and won again with another birdie at the next.

I rounded the turn in 32 strokes and was three up on Chick. He came back a little in the last nine, but I held on to my lead and won the Championship, 2 and 1.

That was my greatest shot in golf and that was my greatest moment in golf.

In looking back on my years in golf, starting in 1931 when I won the State Championship in Sydney, Australia at the age of 16, I feel my "greatest moment in golf" has to be the day I won the P.G.A. Championship in Detroit. Every professional wants to have his name engraved on the big P.G.A. cup. It seems to repay with personal satisfaction all the hours spent on the practice tee and the big decision to turn professional.

(s) Jim Ferrier

12
Doug Ford

It was in March 1957 at the National Golf Show in New York City when Doug Ford came to the *Golf World* Magazine booth (with whom I was unofficially working) to cast his selection of the Master's Tournament Winner. Lillian Harlow, *Golf World* Magazine publisher, had posted a Savings Bond prize to be awarded to the person who could guess the winner and the winning score of the forthcoming Masters Tournament. Doug Ford was the only professional to select himself to win and he guessed that a 283 score would win. Moments later, Jack Burke, Jr. (and I shall never forget his bronze tan fresh from the sunny grapefruit circuit), the reigning Masters Champion, came by and saw Ford's selection. Stated Jack, "Doug could very well be the winner, such damn confidence and positive thinking are the requisites to win any title."

A few weeks later, Doug Ford hit his approach shot in the trap adjacent to the 18th green in the final round of the Masters Tournament. Doug had just made his 282nd stroke and he was in the lead. However, in order to win, score-wise, he had to sink his explosion shot, a most difficult feat—he did.

In the following year, Doug Ford came within a whisker of successfully defending his title, but some rookie professional by the name of Arnold Palmer squeezed him out by a single stroke. The name of this rookie professional was to reappear again and again.

And who will ever forget the finals of the National PGA Championship in 1955 at the Meadowbrook Country Club in Detroit. During this torrid heat wave which broke all the weather records since the settlers claimed Michigan from the Indians, Doug Ford, the swift swinger and the fastest player in the history of golf, was to match strokes with Cary Middlecoff, the most deliberate player the game has ever known. On the eve of the finals, the experts had voted Middlecoff the victor by 13 to 1. Said one golf writer who possessed one of the most analytical minds of all, "Doug cannot possibly change his rapid pace and produce the shots required to defeat the Doctor." Said another, who even laid the odds in cash, "This is Doug's first attempt in the PGA Championship and Cary is a proven seasoned veteran in major

Doug Ford, one of the fastest players in the game, cuts loose with a wedge. Doug won the National PGA Championship in 1955 at the Meadowbrook Country Club, Michigan, where he set a torrid pace from the very beginning and played 194 holes in 39 strokes below par. In 1957, he won the prestigious Masters Tournament when he holed a trap-shot on the final green. A native of New York, Doug was one of the leading money winners on tour. (Photo by MacGregor)

Doug Ford prepares to blast from the trap adjacent to the 9th green during the 1970 Masters Tournament. It was this type of shot which Doug executed in winning the 1957 Masters title. He holed out from a trap at the 18th green for a birdie-3 to score a 66 and the victory. (Photo by Nevin H. Gibson)

championships." Someone else volunteered to quote, "How many times has a Medalist ever won the finals in a match play championship?" Further discussions revealed most explicitly that a fast Yankee could not possibly defeat a slow Rebel in this heat and poor Doug would be "fiddlecoffed" to defeat. Since this was my first PGA Championship, where I posed as a scribe, I only listened, but I got the message and obviously joined the 13 experts.

It was apparent that Mr. Douglas M. Ford had other ideas. He had waited five long years to become eligible to play in this event even though he had already proved his supremacy. And if I recall correctly, Doug was somewhat bitter about this requirement. So it came to pass the next day when Doug equipped himself with a folding chair, the right pace and most important, the correct strokes to become victorious by 4 and 3.

It was earlier, in fact in 1953, when Doug Ford was elected as the most improved professional golfer of the year. His earnings had increased from $14,566.19 to $26,815.50. Two years later, Doug proved the voters to be correct as he became the PGA Player of the Year, and for every year over one decade, he has been in the top ten leading money winners bracket. In spite of the recent inflated purses, at the end of 1968 he ranked #10 as the all-time leading money winner.

Among Doug Ford's 19 official tournament victories, surpassed only by Arnold Palmer, Jack Nicklaus, Billy Casper and Gene Littler (of the still active players), are one Masters, one PGA Championship, two Canadian Opens, one Western Open and one Eastern Open. As recently as August 30, 1970, Doug Ford scored a 284, four under par, to tie Jack Nicklaus and Billy Casper in the Dow Jones Open to win $4,833.

All-Time Professional Record:

TOUR VICTORIES: 1952—Jacksonville Open. 1953—Virginia Beach Open, Labatt Open, Miami Open. 1954—Greensboro Open, Fort Wayne Open. 1955—PGA Championship, All-American, Carling Open. 1957—Los Angeles Open, Masters, Western Open. 1958—Pensacola Open. 1959— Canadian Open. 1960—Indianapolis "500" Festival Open. 1961—Indianapolis "500" Festival Open. 1962—Crosby National, Eastern Open. 1963—Canadian Open.

MONEY RECORD:

1950	$ 2,918.83	1960	$28,411.57
1951	11,005.58	1961	26,677.39
1952	14,566.19	1962	28,041.98
1953	26,815.50	1963	25,895.09
1954	16,415.84	1964	8,063.68
1955	33,503.92	1965	12,559.46
1956	19,389.58	1966	7,685.72
1957	45,378.56	1967	21,246.67
1958	21,874.87	(Thru '67	Total $381,406.38)
1959	31,009.95		

Douglas M. Ford relates his greatest moment in golf:

My "greatest moment in golf" was the winning of the PGA Championship in 1955. My reason for this feeling is that it was my first Major Title and was won under grueling conditions.

I won the Qualifying Medal, a 36 holes medal, and then played match play, finally winning 4 and 3 on the 33rd hole. We played for seven days in heat and humidity that set records in Detroit for that time of the year.

It was the first time I was eligible to play in the Championship as I had to wait five years to become a Class A professional. Only Class A Members are able to play in the PGA Championship. This requirement was lifted in 1958 when the event changed to stroke play.

(s) Doug Ford

13
Al Geiberger

Al Geiberger, a pencil-slender, 6′ 2½″ product of California was a collegian at the University of Southern California and had a 34–2 record thereat. He twice won the Pacific Coast Conference title, twice the Southern California Intercollegiate title and was the National Jaycee Champion in 1954.

Al became a professional in 1959 and during the decade of the 1960's, his "Tournament Play Average" was 71.316 per round. Although he has won only four official PGA tour victories, his record is fantastic. He was runnerup eleven times and on seven occasions, he finished third. During this period he won $406,699.06 in official PGA earnings which places him well among the top with the all-time leading money winners. This does not include his victories and earnings in the two televised CBS Golf Classics, which he won with Dave Stockton, and the Caracas Open victory on the Caribbean tour.

Al played on the U.S. Ryder Cup team in 1967 and during this year he played in 24 tournaments, completed 24 and collected prize money in 24 and ended the year with earnings of $63,315.20.

At the 1970 Masters tournament, Al just made the cut at 150, and while lunching with him and his wife Judy, he related his thrills and his greatest moment in golf:

The Firestone Country Club in Akron, Ohio, has provided me with three great thrills which may be considered as great moments in golf. Ironically, one of my saddest moments occurred after I won the 1966 National PGA Championship thereat. Television was black-out in the Akron area, and a short period later, in Canton, Ohio, when I was watching the delayed replay on TV, a newscast came over announcing the tragic airplane crash which took the life of my friend Tony Lema and his wife.

My first thrill at the Firestone Country Club occurred in 1965 when I won the American Golf Classic. I held a 5 stroke lead going into the last round. I ended up winning by four shots. The thrill was winning on one of the toughest courses in the country against as strong a field as you'll find.

My second thrill and great moment happened in the year following when I captured the 1966 National PGA Championship. I shared the lead after the first round with Sam Snead when we scored a pair of 68's. I lost my lead on the second day but came back on the third with another 68 and led by four shots. Then in the last round, I bogied the first two holes, parred the third and bogied the fourth. On the par-3 fifth hole, I dropped a 25-foot putt which really gave me the boost I needed. When you start bad and go three over on the first four holes, how can you get back on the rugged Firestone Course? What a shock! But this long putt came at a crucial time to give me the confidence I needed. After I made my par on the 16th hole, I knew then that I had won the National PGA Championship. My principal objective which I concentrated on was to get through the 16th hole. You can imagine the elations I experienced when I conquered this task. It was a great feeling to know that I could six putt the final hole and still win the PGA Championship. I am sure every professional dreams of winning the National PGA title and I was most thrilled to accomplish this feat. Other factors which made this victory more important was the fact that it was played over a rugged championship course. Also, my poor start in the final round challenged me to exert a psychological frame from which I knew I must produce my best physical potential in order to win. When I achieved this, I knew that I would never be considered as a "flash" winner. It was indeed a great honor to win this most prestigious championship under the conditions which existed.

My third great thrill came the next year, 1967, which extended through 1968 when Dave Stockton and I won the CBS Golf Classic and successfully defended our title in 1968. Dave and I won a record of ten straight victories before we bowed in defeat in the semifinals in 1970. These most popular matches are televised and are arranged whereas leading money winners on the tour are paired and compete against another twosome in an elimination match-play event. Therefore the competition becomes very keen which makes these events most popular with the television exposure. It was indeed a great thrill to win these two consecutive Classics which established a record.

Another great thrill I experienced was in 1959 before I became a professional. During this period I won eleven amateur titles in a row then I entered the Los Angeles Open Championship. I was obviously anxious to see how I would fare against the top professionals. During the last day I was paired with Arnold Palmer and I scored my lowest round, a 69, while Arnie took a 72 and I ended with a 283 in a tie for fifth place. Naturally, playing in my native area made this performance more important. Ken Venturi, another Californian, was victorious with a 278. This tournament convinced me that I could

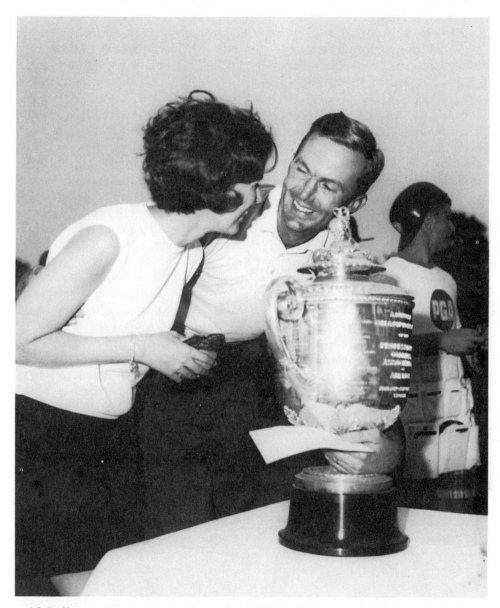

Al Geiberger and wife Judy with a $25,000 check and trophy after win-
ning the National PGA Championship in 1966 at the Firestone Country
Club, in Akron, Ohio. Al has amassed an outstanding record over the
rugged Firestone Course. He won the American Golf Classic there in
1965 and teamed with Dave Stockton, they won two consecutive CBS
Golf Classics there in 1967 and 1968. (Photo by Firestone)

compete with the top professionals and it was certainly a great moment and I shall always remember January 5, 1959.

As insignificant as it may appear, my "greatest moment in golf" occurred when I was a Junior at the University of Southern California in 1958 when I was the number 4 man on the team, and at the age of 20. The prestigious Palm Springs Invitational Amateur Championship played at the O'Donnell Golf Course, the first course in Palm Springs, sent me an invitation to participate. It was during Easter Vacation and the invited competitors were the leading amateurs at the time, which included: Harvie Ward, Bruce McCormick, Johnny Dawson, Dr. Bud Taylor, etc. Ken Venturi and Gene Littler were previous contenders before they turned professional. As indicated by the elite list of invited amateurs, this was one of the most important Amateur Invitational Championships in the U.S. which was decided by stroke play. It was an honor just to be invited to play in this event. Compounding the importance of this event was the fact that I had not been playing well the last two years since I left Junior golf and I was sincerely doubtful whether I had what it took. I was most elated when I finished in a tie with Bruce McCormick. Bruce was a veteran amateur golfer and had won practically every amateur title on the West Coast. When I defeated Bruce in a play-off under grueling pressure, it was definitely my "greatest moment in golf." This play-off victory gave me the confidence and the assurance that I could match strokes with the best. This was actually the turning point in my golfing career. Immediately after this victory I was advanced to the number one man on the University's team. My game continued to improve from then on. I have been very fortunate in golf and the game has been very good to me. Winning the National PGA Championship, apart from the 25 grand in prize money, was a great honor in values other than monetary and I am certainly proud of this great achievement. However, this victory, like all the others, is contributable to that day in 1958 when I won the Palm Springs Invitational Amateur Championship which gave me the necessary confidence I required to pursue this career.

14
Nevin H. Gibson

In response to my request to the leading golfers of the world for a narrative of their "greatest moments in golf," a few of the leaders responded with the same question to me. In reply, my first impulse was to relate the story when I dropped a most difficult down-hill putt on the 18th green of the old Broadmoor Golf Course in Colorado Springs in 1951 for my record score of 69. Not only did this 69 establish my record but it enabled me to defeat a group of wealthy Texans which heretofore seemed impossible.

In this particular match with my sub-par round in progress, naturally, all bets were pressed on the 18th tee. Consequently, a par-four would be of little value under the circumstances as I had already scored a number of 70's, which was my record at the time. Therefore, the birdie-putt was very important and when it dropped, you can surmise my great elation.

These hustlers migrated to the Springs every Summer to escape the Texas heat and played golf every day. They were outstanding golfers and they could and usually shot par golf, obviously having a great advantage over the working tribe. In fact, for a longer period than I care to remember, I was the victim paying their expenses and these characters lived high on the hog. Finally, our professional, the late Ed Dudley, called me aside and gave me a lesson on the psychological aspect of the game. Therefore, my incredible 69 was partially contributable to Ed Dudley. I may add at this point, the very next day my score of 70 was more of a financial asset than the 69. (These clowns had doubled the stakes.) These great scores did have their disadvantages, as it became increasingly difficult for me to arrange a decent game with those Texans thereafter.

My greatest moment, however, was not on a golf course but somewhat connected with golf. I was covering the 1967 U.S. Open Championship at the Baltusrol Golf Club in Springfield, New Jersey, and I called home prior to the third round of play. My wife reported that our middle son, Byron, then 19, had had a most serious motorcycle accident. He had, among other things a fractured skull and

Jack Nicklaus, the "Golden Bear," reputed to be the world's greatest golfer, poses with the author at the famed Merion Golf Club, Oakmont, Pennsylvania, prior to his play-off for the 1971 U.S. Open Championship title. It was a coincidence that one of Jack's greatest moments in golf occurred during the same tournament when the author experienced a most tragic—then his greatest—moment. (Photo by "Red" Hoffman, *Newark* (NJ) *News*)

had been under surgery at the Walter Reed Hospital in Washington, D. C., for seven hours and may not live. Without packing, I drove home immediately. Foremost in my mind was to see Byron before he died. At this point I thought if my son did live, he may never regain his normal mental faculties. I thought of a million things including, most of all, those things a father should have done for his son. Byron had tried to sell the bike upon my request and it was advertised in the *Washington Post* for one week, but this effort was in vain, he received no sale.

Finally, I arrived at the hospital after grinding through five hours of Saturday traffic on the Garden State Highway which seemed a lifetime. When I entered my son's room, Byron opened his eyes, smiled, raised his hand to shake and said, "Hi, Dad." This was indeed the greatest moment in my life. Eight days later, Byron was up and mean as ever. Naturally, I thanked the great surgeons and the Almighty.

15
Bob Goalby

One may wonder if Bob Goalby, the versatile athlete, pursued the career in which he is best qualified. He was a four sport athlete at Belleville High School and won eleven letters. Three major league baseball teams were interested in Bob but he went to the University of Illinois where he played one season of football as a reserve quarterback and a defensive regular. Later, as an automobile salesman, he won a half dozen amateur golf tournaments from 1953 through 1956 before turning professional at the age of 26 in 1957.

Bob's first professional victory came in 1958 when he won the Greater Greensboro Open and was named the "Rookie of the Year." The handsome professional had a great year in 1961 when he won the Los Angeles Open and the St. Petersburg Open. In winning the St. Petersburg event, he registered a most phenomenal achievement of making eight consecutive birdies, establishing an all-time record which still stands today. Bob scored these birdies in the last round.

Another great year followed when in 1962 Bob won the Insurance City Open after a sudden-death play-off with Art Wall which ended on the seventh extra hole. One month later he captured the Denver Open. Earlier in the year during the National PGA Championship at the classy Aronimink course near Philadelphia, Bob brought the tournament to a thrilling climax and made a courageous bid for the title. With Gary Player leading by three strokes and playing in the same threesome, Bob dropped a 20-foot putt for a birdie on the 14th and got another at the par-5 16th to end with a brilliant 67 for a 279 total, but Player's 278 won the title by a single stroke. Gary became the first foreign citizen to win the National PGA Championship.

In 1963, Bob played on the U.S. Ryder Cup team and won both his matches, then he went into a slump which lasted through four seasons during which nothing seemed to go right. Finally, in 1967, he came back strong and won the San Diego Open when he blasted from a trap on the last hole and dropped the putt for his victory. Bob had nine finishes in the top ten and ended the year with official earnings

Bob Goalby, the handsome professional from Illinois, holds the record of scoring eight consecutive birdies in a PGA Tour event. Bob amassed this record in the final round of the St. Petersburg Open in 1961 and won with a closing 65. Bob was tied for second in the 1961 U.S. Open Championship and in the following year, he was a runner-up in the National PGA Championship. However, Bob reaped a heavy harvest in 1968 when he finally captured a major title by winning the prestigious Masters Tournament. Bob played on the U.S. Ryder Cup Team in 1963 and was a member of the PGA Tournament Committee from 1962 through 1964. (Photo by Spalding)

of $77,106.85. Says Jack Nicklaus, "Bob, the self-taught golfer—did not quit the tour in disgust, as most men would have. He stuck with it and fought his way back. It took a lot of courage."

In the following year, Bob had one of his greatest, if not his greatest, moments in golf when he captured the coveted title of the prestigious Masters Tournament. In the final round, Bob made a charge on the back nine when he birdied the 13th and 14th, then he made a brilliant eagle on the 5-par 15th to score a 277 total to finally win his first major title.

Things went bad for Bob after his Master's victory when he went through almost two seasons without a tour win and faced the requirement of qualifying on Mondays but he came through to win the Robinson Open in his native state. Again, he went through 14 months without a victory and faced the same situation but late in 1970 he won the Heritage Classic in Hilton Head Island, South Carolina with a final round 66 for a four stroke victory margin. This was Bob's eleventh professional tour victory which brought his all-time official PGA earnings to $471,154.81. (This does not include the oversight of $20 which Bob won in his first PGA tally, "Mayfair Inn Open Invitational" at Sanford, Florida, in December of 1957 when he shot a final round of 64 to get into the money bracket with a total score of 283.)

In summation, Bob's tournament stroke play average was 71.338 strokes per round. He won eleven, was runnerup 16 times and on 11 occasions, he finished third. This record places Mr. Goalby in number 7 position among the "Leading Tournament Finishers" during his professional career. This record is most amazing, considering those scabrous seasons which Bob endured.

Bob Goalby relates his greatest moments in golf:

Regarding my "greatest moments in golf," actually, I have had two of them. The first occurred in 1961 in the final round of the St. Petersburg Open. I was fortunate enough to make eight consecutive birdies. The streak began on number Eight and ended on the 15th hole. The eight birdies in a row is an all-time PGA record. I won the golf tournament with a final round of 65.

Also a great moment in golf for me was in the Masters Golf Tournament in 1968. Winning the Masters was possibly the "greatest moment in golf" for me. The 15th hole in the final round possibly provided as much thrill for me as actually winning. I played a three-iron second shot to the par-five green—this is a small and normally firm green. The shot was probably the finest long iron I had ever hit. The ball grazed the putting surface and stopped very quickly about eight feet below the hole. This shot, along with making the putt, enabled me to get in position to win the tournament.

I believe that at that moment, walking off the 15th green, I had a feeling of more elation than at any other time in my golf career.

(s) Bob Goalby

16
Ralph Guldahl

In the era following the reign of Bobby Jones, Walter Hagen, Gene Sarazen and their contemporaries, came one Ralph Guldahl. Ralph and his counterparts Byron Nelson, Sam Snead and Ben Hogan were destined to write a new chapter in the history of American golf.

The phenomenal golf records established by Ralph Guldahl have been properly recorded and will remain in the historical records of golf forever. However, the voluminous stories told about Ralph's rise to fame and glory have varied most considerably. In a precise and accurate narrative, Ralph, a native Texan, made his first notable mark in golf as an amateur in the Dallas City Championship at the age of 17 in 1929. In the semi-finals of this event he defeated Gus Moreland and in the finals, none other than "Spec" Goldman, one of the foremost amateurs in Texas. This convinced Ralph that he could compete with the best and was perhaps his first great moment in golf.

In 1930 Ralph became a professional. During these days an amateur could declare himself as competing for the prize money before teeing off in the final round. In which case, he lost his amateur status and became a professional. It was under these circumstances that Ralph, standing in fourth place and prior to teeing off in the last round, decided to compete for the money which automatically made him a professional. Ralph then shot his poorest round, a 76, over the easy Breckenridge course in San Antonio to win $100 in a tie for 11th place. A good round would have won him $400 to $600. After the Texas Open, Ralph returned to Dallas as a professional at a small club and saved his money for the tour. He joined the tour in September, 1930. It so happened that Ralph, with another Texan, Ben Hogan, drove up to St. Louis and entered the $10,000 Open. Ralph led the field after the first round with a 66, six under par, then finished with 75–73–71 and tied for ninth to win $200.

In 1931, Ralph won his first tournament, which was the $5,000 Motion Picture Match Play Championship at the Riviera Country Club in Los Angeles during January, winning $1,000. In April, during the same year, Ralph married.

Ralph Guldahl executes a perfect trap shot. Within a short span of three years, 1936 to 1939, this Dallas native was "untouchable." He won two consecutive U.S. Open titles, one Masters Tournament and three consecutive Western Open Championships. (Photo by D. Scott Chisholm)

Ralph won his second tournament in 1932 when he captured the Phoenix Open. In the year following, he gained nine strokes on nine holes on Johnny Goodman in the final round of the U.S. Open Championship, only to miss a four-foot putt on the final green to lose to the amateur. After this tragic miss to fame and glory, not to mention the money, his game suffered. During this lapse he left the tour. He tried selling automobiles. He sold one—the one he purchased. Ralph returned to Dallas in 1935 and later drove to Los Angeles where he played poorly. With his wife and son both down sick, he completely gave up the game and took a job as a stage hand. With his wife's encouragement, Ralph borrowed money and returned to the PGA tour which was then under the direction of Freddy Corcoran. In his first start, Ralph ended in 8th place in the True Temper Open to win $600 and Ralph Guldahl was on his way. He arrived in Davenport, Iowa, and shot a final round of 64 to win his first of three consecutive Western Open Championships and by the end of the year, he had won three more tournaments, was the second leading money winner and won the Radix Cup with a scoring average of 71.63.

In the year following, Ralph appeared to be the sure winner of the Masters title with a three stroke lead at the turn. He birdied the 10th but he had troubles on the 12th and 13th where Byron Nelson gained six strokes to win his first major golf title. Ralph was to start his dominating reign a short period later.

Just two months after Ralph's tragic defeat in the Master's event of 1937, he arrived at the Oakland Hills Country Club in Birmingham, Michigan to vie for the U.S. Open Championship. Sam Snead, the favorite of the gallery, playing in his first U.S. Open Championship, finished with a most respectful 283, just one stroke over the record. Ralph was on the green of the 5-par eighth hole in two, 25 feet from the hole, when he heard of Snead's record finish over the loudspeaker. After combing his hair he then crouched over the ball in his characteristic stance, and stroked it in the center of the hole for an eagle-3 when he needed it most. He hit a crisp one iron shot on the 190-yard ninth hole, eight feet from the pin for his birdie and rounded the turn three under par. Ralph bogied both the 10th and 11th holes but came back with birdies on the 12th and 13th and parred the remaining holes to finish with a blazing 69 for a 281 record score to win his first major championship. During the same year, he won his second consecutive Western Open title, was runner-up in five other events and won both his matches in the Ryder Cup event in England.

Back at the Masters in Augusta, Georgia, in 1938, Ralph playing with the immortal Bobby Jones. He started the last round with a par eagle-birdie and turned with a 34, then he birdied the 15th but three-putted the 16th and 18th to end as a runner-up for the second straight year. It was a different story at the Cherry Hills Country Club in Denver, the venue for the U.S. Open Championship, where Ralph arrived to defend his title. Defend it he did by picking up ten strokes on the faltering Dick Metz in the last round and again he finished with an incredible 69 to win by six strokes and become the fourth man in history to win two consecutive U.S. Open Championships. Just a few days later at the Westwood Country Club in St. Louis, Ralph fired a closing round of 65 to become the first and only man in history to win three consecutive Western Open titles.

It was in 1939 back to the Masters, where Ralph Guldahl had been runner-up during the two previous years, that he made another indelible mark on the records of golf. The first day's play was washed out and 36 holes were scheduled for Sunday. After two rounds, Gene Sarazen held a one stroke lead over Ralph and Sam Snead who were tied at 140. On Sunday, 8,000 spectators, a record number, watched the final 36 holes of play. After the first round, Ralph's 70 gave him

The author, left, and Ralph Guldahl pose at the Augusta National Golf Club during the 1971 Masters Tournament. It was here, 32 years earlier, that Ralph won the Masters title in one of the most thrilling tournaments in the history of the Masters. (Photo by Bill Davis, *Golf Digest***)**

a 210 total for a one stroke lead over Sarazen while a host of the world's best, comprising Snead, Burke, Little and "Lord" Byron Nelson, were grouped at 212. In the last and final round when Ralph made the turn at the ninth hole, Snead had just holed out on the nearby 18th with a most brilliant 68 to establish a new Master's record of 280. Ralph finished the first nine in even par-36, and the huge gallery left Snead to follow Ralph and Lawson Little, who were tied. On the 10th green, after the crowd settled, Ralph replaced his comb in his pocket and stooped his 200-pound frame over the ball in his characteristic style and dropped his putt for a birdie-3. Lawson missed a 3-footer for his par.

Ralph parred the 11th and 12th. On the 13th hole, he drove about 220 yards down the middle but he had a most difficult lie. In order to get home in two, which he knew he must in order to catch Snead, he needed a terrific carry of some 230 yards to clear the creek in front of the green. Ralph selected a 3-wood and slammed it. The ball carried over the water and stopped six feet from the pin. It was indeed a shot of a master. He made his eagle-3, then shot 4–4–3–5–4 to score a 69 which established a record 279 to win. It was the third time Ralph finished with a 69 to win a major championship. It was also the second time he knocked out Sam Snead in a major championship.

Ralph's most deliberate play and his nature of keeping to himself did not make him popular with the gallery or his fellow professionals. He frequently stopped to comb his hair and fiddled around before executing his shot according to his opponents. He was not a Walter Hagen or Arnold Palmer in any sense of the imagination. He was not magnetic in personality and obviously this did not appeal to the public. However, he could and did play superb golf which added tremendously to the game in many aspects. About this hair combing bit, Ralph stated: "It checks my pace and helps me to retain that confident composure."

Ralph Guldahl relates his greatest moment in golf:

My greatest moment in golf came as a result of the greatest and most exceptional golf shot I ever executed which enabled me to win the Master's Title in 1939. This most prestigious Championship had escaped my grasp on two previous occasions when I thought I had it won but I ended as a runner-up.

In the final round when I walked off the ninth green Sam Snead had just finished the 18th hole with a record score of 280. I was playing with Lawson Little and as we approached the tenth hole I knew I needed a 34 on the back nine to tie and a 33 to win. The huge gallery had left Snead to join Lawson and me on the tenth. It was actually this hole which set me up for a chance or a feeling that I could win.

After my drive I hit a 4-iron shot seven feet from the hole and dropped the putt for a birdie. I then parred 11 and hit a six iron seven feet from the flag at 12. Although I missed my birdie, I was satisfied with a par-3. This hole had cost me the title in 1937. On the 13th, my drive was down the middle about 225 yards but it left me with a most difficult lie which was slightly down and sidehill and rather snug. It was some 245 yards from the flag and required a carry of about 235 yards to clear the embankment of the creek which ran in front of the green. My first thought was should I play short, then pitch up close for a possible birdie? It seemed an eternity for me to decide. Then I realized in order to catch Snead I had to go for everything. I selected a number 3 wood and cut across the ball to get it up from the tight lie. The ball hit just 10 feet beyond the creek and stopped within six feet of the hole. What a sensation I had when I followed the flight of this most beautiful shot that went dead to the flag. The crowd screamed. It was indeed my greatest moment in golf. I knew then that this shot paved the way for my victory. It is most difficult to describe the feeling I had. It was a gamble to some extent as the shot had to be executed perfectly in order to obtain the desired results. This did not assure my victory but it gave me more confidence to play the remaining holes in par, which would give me the victory. I got my par at 14 and on the 5-par 15th I went for the green and my ball stopped 45 feet from the hole. I got down in two for a birdie-4. On the old 3-par 16th I hit a six iron about seven feet from the hole but I missed my birdie. On the 17th after a perfect drive I was afraid of burying my ball in the trap and over-clubbed. From behind the green I chipped with an eight iron within five feet but missed my par. After a fair drive on the 18th I made a club change for my approach. I used a four iron and was 15 feet behind the hole on the rear of the green. I nudged the putt within six inches of the hole and it was at this point that I realized I was definitely the winner of this prestigious Masters Tournament. Naturally, I contribute this victory to that second shot on the 13th.

(s) Ralph Guldahl

17
Paul Harney

Paul Harney joined the professional ranks late in 1954, a few months after his discharge from the U.S. Navy. Despite his slight build, 5′ 11½″, and 150 pounds, he is one of the longest hitters in the game. It was coincidental that two other long hitters, Arnold Palmer and Big George Bayer, arrived on the scene during the same year.

Paul's first professional victory came in 1956 when he won the Egyptian PGA Championship. It was however in the following year when he won his first official PGA Tour event. Going into the last round of play, Paul was tied with Arnold Palmer, one stroke behind Bert Weaver, in the Carlings Open at Flint, Michigan. Then Harney shot a closing 68 for a nine under par, 275, which won the tournament by three strokes. In the following week at Detroit, he missed by one stroke to participate in the playoff for the Western Open Championship. Then one week later, Paul won his second official PGA tour title at Montreal where he was victorious in the Labatt Open. By the end of 1957, Paul ranked as the sixth leading money winner and he earned the award as the Most Improved Professional in 1957.

Late in 1958, the prodigious hitter won the Dorado Beach Invitation at Puerto Rico and in the following year, he won the Pensacola Open when he scored a blazing 269 total to win by three strokes.

After eight years on the pro tour, the ex-caddy from Worcester, Massachusetts, accepted a club position (in order to devote more time to his family) which limited his appearance on the tournament circuit. In spite of Paul's infrequent play and cutting his swing down at a sacrifice of distance, he continued to hold his own on the professional tour when he participated.

In the first tournament of 1964, the Los Angeles Open, Paul trailed Bob Nichols and Tommy Jacobs by seven strokes after the second round, then closed with 66–71 for a 280 total to win over Nichols by one stroke. One year later, he successfully defended his title when he finished with a most brilliant 276 over the same course. In the year to follow, 1966, Paul finished again with a 276 but it placed him second to Arnold Palmer, the winner.

Paul Harney salutes the gallery after winning his second consecutive Los Angeles Open title in 1965 on the final green of the Rancho Golf Course. Paul grew up across the street from the Tatnuck Golf Course in Worcester, Massachusetts, and developed his game by sneaking onto the course at night. (Photo from Paul Harney)

The religious Harney, most congenial and one of the most likable professionals, has consistently surprised the golfing world with his calibre of performance as a part-time touring professional. He has time and time again come from nowhere to vie in the top of contention. As recent as September, 1970, this son of a retired Worcester police sergeant finished second in the Greater Hartford Open to win $11,813.39 and his official PGA earnings for the year exceeded $40,000.

In January of 1971 after the third round in the Phoenix Open, Paul's 194 was 19 strokes under par and he led Gene Littler by one stroke for the lead. However, Miller Barber slid in with a final 65 to win. It was just one week later in the Andy Williams-San Diego Open when Paul arrived at the par-3 sixteenth hole, ten under par in the final round. The 16th was the "hole in one" hole and the closest to the hole was awarded a new automobile. When Paul split the flag with his tee shot, the excited TV commentator announced that Paul was the winner. However, after computations by the computer, he lost by three inches. Nevertheless, Paul Harney's eleven under par was good for a tie at third place and $7,313.

It was on January 30, 1972, when Paul Harney, again at the Andy Williams-San Diego Open, hit a 4-wood approach onto the green of the 501-yard 5-par final hole and two-putted for a birdie to win $30,000 by a single stroke. Paul's victory is most incredible in view of the fact that he hasn't toured regularly since 1962.

Before Paul became a professional and a lieutenant in the U.S. Navy, he was the Captain of the Holy Cross College golf team. He won 52 of the 56 matches and was the Medalist in the 1952 NCAA Tournament. During the same year, he won the Eastern Intercollegiate Championship.

Paul Harney relates his greatest moment in golf:

It was a high sunny day in Flint, Michigan, on the 18th green at Flint Country Club, the site of the Carlings Open in 1957, which brings back the exciting memories. I suppose every touring pro's ambition initially is to prove that he is better than everyone else; that is to win a tournament. This actually was my goal.

As I walked up to the last hole of the tournament, I can still remember being utterly confused as to how I stood with the rest of the field. I knew I was probably leading but as to how many strokes, I did not have the faintest idea. When our threesome arrived at the 18th green, I stood and watched Dow Finsterwald hole about a 50-foot putt and the thought went through my mind that maybe he was now even with me.

I don't even recall hitting my 20 foot putt. I do remember quite vividly of looking up in time to see the putt going toward and finally dropping in the middle of the hole. When being congratulated later,

I knew for certain I had won. This certainly has to be one of my "great moments of golf."

(s) Paul Harney

18
Dave Hill

Reputed as the world's most controversial golfer, Dave Hill is perhaps the most dedicated golfer, in his quest to become a perfectionist, than any professional on the Tour. His greatest concern is becoming technically correct in every movement of his swing. Dave became a professional in 1958 and is one of the few who receives as much enjoyment from his practice sessions as when playing.

He strives to master the ball like Ben Hogan and to swing like Sam Snead. He is most determined in his goals· "I want to play golf as good as I can play for as long as I can play."

In spite of Dave's serious endeavor to master the game, he is best known for his provocative off-beat quotes, saying precisely what he thinks regardless of the time, place or circumstance. It would appear that such down-right honesty would be an asset but Dave has received more penalties and paid more fines than any player on the Tour.

During the decade of the 1960's, Dave won $365,450.23 in official PGA earnings. He won seven tournaments, was runner-up six times and on six occasions he finished third. In 1969, he won three events and, most important, he won the prestigious Vardon Trophy, signifying the lowest scoring average (70.344) of the year, as well as earning a berth on the Ryder Cup team.

Dave continued his remarkable pace in the 1970's by winning the Danny Thomas Memphis Classic the third time in a four-year span. He finished second in the U.S. Open Championship. Dave played in 25 events in 1970 and won an average of $14,736 in each tournament while his scoring average of 70.78 placed him second for the Vardon Trophy award.

Just recently, the brash, out-spoken Hill was voted the game's most colorful golfer by the Golf Writers Association when its members were polled to choose the man who brought the most flair, charisma and performance to the game. Said one of the voters, "He has the fire, drive and desire and he can play like hell."

Dave Hill's greatest moment in golf, as related by Oscar Fraley:
If there has been one outstanding moment in my golf career to date

Dave Hill poses on the practice tee. He is one of the few golfers who receives as much enjoyment from his practice sessions as when playing. Dave's greatest concern is becoming technically correct in every movement of his swing. Dave won three Tour events in 1969 and the prestigious Vardon Trophy. (Photo by RAM)

Dave Hill, the most colorful golfer of 1969, swings from the 10th tee during the 4th round of the Westchester Classic of 1970 at New York. Dave birdied the last hole to tie for fifth place. (Photo by Nevin H. Gibson)

I'd have to guess that it was the day I won the 1969 Buick Open at Flint, Michigan. The primary reason is that I was born in Jackson, Michigan, and it seemed to me as if everybody from my home town was on hand for the final round.

I'm not one of those silver spoon kids. My dad was a postal worker and I don't have to tell you a man with a family buys more beans than caviar on that kind of salary. We kids were expected to pitch in and help where we could and I was caddying as soon as I could tote a bag.

I'd turned pro in 1959 and I'd won a few tournaments like the Home of the Sun Open and the Denver Open in 1961, the Hot Springs Open in 1963 and the Memphis Open in 1967 and earlier again in 1969. But I hadn't really set the world on fire and I'd been through a couple of years where I was sick and I needed to prove something to myself.

So here was my chance to do it—and in front of a lot of folks from my home town who remembered me as that "skinny little Hill kid."

I held the lead going into the final round and it's a spot where you just might find yourself looking back over your shoulder so often that you'll let your shots get away from you, start pressing and blow the whole deal. And they were after me.

Dave Hill receives a pictorial engraved plaque from Gordon Johnson. Voted as the golfer who brought the most flair, charisma and performance to the game, Dave has the "fire, drive and desire" and, as one voter stated, "he can play like hell." (Photo by Pittsburgh Paints)

First, Lee Elder made a run at me and fell back. Then it was Homero Blancas but I held him off. And coming down the final fairway the only man who had a shot at me was Frank Beard.

I knocked it down the middle and looking back saw Beard standing on the tee waiting to hit his drive. So I decided to strap a little gamesmanship on him. I took plenty of time selecting a club, walked up toward the green for a look at the pin placement, walked back and picked another club and generally wasted time while Frank was striding back and forth on the tee waiting to make a drive that might get him a tying birdie. Finally, with great deliberation, I hit my shot to the green and moved out of range. Then I went about the business of getting my par and he could do no better than match it.

I wouldn't be surprised if they could hear those Jackson people yelling all the way back home as I accepted the winner's check. That "little skinny Hill kid" had pulled it off for them.

A great moment, yes, considering the circumstances. And yet, whether it is in a tournament or on the practice tee, my greatest moments are when I strike the ball exactly the way I want to hit it. I am obsessed with the idea of being very correct technically. I can't settle for mediocrity and that makes me my own worst enemy.

Maybe it sounds silly, but I do not care if I win one tournament or a thousand but I do want to master a golf ball the way Ben Hogan masters it. I do not play tournaments thinking of the money I might win. I want to play to the best of my ability and that means hitting the shots in the manner they should be hit.

Hitting a shot properly, no matter where or when, is a matchless moment in the life of Dave Hill.

19
Ben Hogan

It was late in August, 1946, in Portland, Oregon, and I was covering my first major golf tournament, the National PGA Championship which was to become the first major golf victory for William Benjamin Hogan. I was mostly concerned at the time with Charlie Congdon, our local Tacoma professional, and Lord Byron Nelson, the defending champion.

During the quarter-finals on the 23rd day of August, Congdon was matched with Harold "Jug" McSpaden and Nelson versus Ed "Porky" Oliver. It was very hot and humid and I was lugging a Speed-graphic camera between the two matches. Charlie Congdon, using a huge bath towel, was constantly wiping the perspiration which was dripping from his face.

When Porky went four or five up on Nelson, I switched to the Congdon–McSpaden match and the "Jughead" eventually won on the 15th green by 5 and 3. I rushed to the Nelson–Oliver match and couldn't believe that Nelson was now one up. I missed his miraculous play where he scored a consecutive string of birdies and an eagle.

I shall never forget the expression and color on Porky's face while he stood on the seventeenth tee. It was actually a reddish-purple and the stress of the toll he endured in this pressure-packed match-play competition was certainly in prominent evidence.

From the 17th tee, Nelson knocked two balls out-of-bounds and the match was even when the pair arrived at the 5-par 18th tee. With my camera loaded, I shot Porky's tee shot after the follow-through and he lost his balance and stumbled forward. Nelson then hit with a perfect follow-through. (Here was my story—I predicted a Nelson victory due to Porky's apparent loss of composure and I had the photographic evidence for proof. However, this story did not materialize because Porky won. Also, I failed to pull the shutter plate before taking the shots.)

Porky played his second shot safely with an iron down the center of the fairway. Nelson went for the green with a wood and pulled the ball to the wooded left rough. At this precise moment, "Jug" McSpaden, his "gold-dust" twin, came running across the fairway from his victory over Congdon to watch Nelson finish. Nelson tossed his club into the air and said, "That was the first time I used that new wood and I should've known better." The two chatted briefly together, then Nelson went to his ball, which was practically unplayable. He managed to extract it to the edge of the rough, and then, from another difficult lie, he played his fourth on the front of the green while Porky was safely on in three, about 15 feet above the hole. Nelson made a courageous effort with the forty-foot putt and the ball hit the center of the hole but bounced out. Porky two-putted for a winning five and Lord Byron Nelson was eliminated.

Although it was a great victory for Ed Oliver, the world of golf expected and was most anxious to see a Nelson–Hogan match, which was not to be. While these described matches were in progress, there were two others in which Hogan defeated Frank Moore by 5 and 4

Ben Hogan experienced his greatest moment in golf during the ticker tape parade given in his honor by New York City in mid-July of 1953, upon his return from Scotland. Ben had just won the British Open Championship (in his first and only attempt) which gave him the third major title during the year, establishing a professional record. (Photo by the *New York Times*)

and Jimmy Demaret defeated Jim Turnesa by 6 and 5.

The next day, Porky defeated Jug McSpaden in the 36-hole semi-finals by 6 and 5, while Hogan defeated Jimmy Demaret by 10 and 9. In the finals, Oliver was two up on Hogan after the morning 18 but Ben came back strong and won by 6 and 4 to capture his first championship on that 25th day of August, 1946. The era of Ben Hogan had just begun.

In 1947, Hogan won seven tour victories and ended as the third leading money winner of the year. In 1948, he captured his first U.S. Open victory, his second PGA Championship, his second Western Open, plus eight other victories. He also won the Vardon Trophy (previously the Radix) for the fifth time and was the year's leading money winner, also for his fifth time.

Ben Hogan won two tournaments early in 1949. Then on a foggy morning, February second, while driving in West Texas enroute to his home in Fort Worth, a huge transcontinental bus plowed head-on into his car. Before the impact, Ben threw himself across his wife's body to protect her. The speedy action saved both lives. The Cadillac was completely demolished and the steering apparatus driven to the rear. His wife, Valerie, suffered only bruises and a black eye. Ben with fractures of the collarbone, pelvis, and left ankle, in addition to chipped ribs, was rushed to the El Paso hospital. The newspapers headlined the tragic accident all over the nation.

The doctors shook their heads sadly. Hogan, they predicted, would be lucky to walk again. Golf was out of question. To make things worse, a blood clot had formed in Ben's left leg and moved to his lungs. A doctor was flown in from New Orleans to perform an emergency operation and Hogan's life was saved. From all indications, Hogan had reached the end of his golfing career.

Few people have ever known the real Ben Hogan. The doctors included. Hogan's great determination, his ability to concentrate, and his serious dedication to the game are the qualitative factors which made him a great golf star. Ben moved to his home in Fort Worth two months after the accident. During his convalescence he thought of many things, and no doubt, his foremost concern was the prospect of pursuing his golf career after he was able to walk.

The golf world was astounded when Ben Hogan appeared on the tee in the Los Angeles Open less than one year after his almost fatal accident. They were shocked even more when he scored a 73 and, still limping from injuries, followed with three consecutive 69s to tie for the lead after Snead sank a difficult curling putt on the last green. Although he lost in the playoff, the important thing was his successful return.

Three months later, he tied Byron Nelson for fourth in the Masters. He reserved his best for the biggest—the U. S. Open at Ardmore, Penn-

This bird's eye view of the 18th green of the Olympic Country Club, San Francisco, the venue for the 1966 U.S. Open Championship, shows Ben Hogan finishing his final round with a most commendable 70 for a 291 total. At this precise time, Palmer was leading Casper by seven strokes at the end of nine holes and Hogan's gallery joined Arnie's army to see Palmer capture his second Open victory. However, Casper gained the deficit and won the play-off. It was here in 1955 when Hogan, seeking his fifth Open victory to become the first and only to win five, lost in a play-off to Jack Fleck. (Photo by Nevin H. Gibson)

sylvania. At the end of four rounds, the gallant little Texan was tied with Lloyd Mangrum and George Fazio for the lead. Still limping from injuries, which became more pronounced as he played, he won the playoff on sheer determination and courage. It was a high point in one of golf's most poignant comebacks.

Hogan continued his mastery in 1951 when he won his first Masters Tournament and successfully defended his U.S. Open title and the world's championship.

It was during this period that a movie, *Follow the Sun*, was made on the life of Ben Hogan. It marked the first and only time that a full-length movie was filmed on a golfer. This great story revealed Ben's desperate struggles during his early career in the professional ranks: his complete failure, his endeavor to return, and his successful triumph after a most determined and dedicated fight. There was only one thing wrong—the movie was made just one year before Ben reached the zenith of his career.

It was in 1953 when Hogan carved out the greatest triumphs of his career by winning the three leading and most prestigious championships of the world. This was the greatest professional feat in the history of golf. He entered five tournaments, apart from the Pro-Ams, and he won them all. This record is more impressive when we realize that Hogan was not playing regularly. He started this most fabulous year at the Augusta National where he again won the Masters Tournament, this time with a record 274. His next victory was in the Pan-American Open. He followed this with a victory at his native Fort Worth, where he won the Colonial National with a 282. Then came the U.S. Open at the rugged Oakmont, where the little man was victorious for his fourth time. His score broke the course record and he was six strokes in front of Sam Snead, the second place finisher. Hogan now turned his sights on the British Open, scheduled at the windswept links of Carnoustie, Scotland, which required a peculiar brand of golf with a smaller ball with which he was not accustomed. Hogan had won every major championship except the British Open in which he never participated. He was openly criticized for not entering this great event prior to 1953. Now he had accepted the challenge. The golfing world was skeptical of his prowess on the ancient windswept links. He opened with a 73 and improved with each round until he scored a final 68 for a 282 to win by four strokes. Yes—it was another record for the Carnoustie course and when the "Wee Ice Mon," as the Scots called him, finished putting on the final hole for his assured victory, there were tears of happiness in the eyes of the golfing world. Ben Hogan had won every major championship of the world.

Ben Hogan relates his greatest moment in golf:

The elation I experienced in the "Ticker Tape Parade" given in my

Desmond "Des" Sullivan, formerly with the *Newark* (NJ) *News* and now retired in Myrtle Beach, South Carolina, describes the drama of Hogan's U.S. Open victory in 1950 at Merion Country Club, Ardmore, Pennsylvania. (Photo by Nevin H. Gibson)

honor by New York City on that mid-July day in 1953 is most difficult to describe.

I thought of many things—my early struggles to succeed back in my home state of Texas—the tremendous support I received from my wife, who encouraged me to continue even during those darkest days—her faith in my ability to succeed, which contributed immeasurably to my success—the almost fatal automobile accident—and of course, my latest victory in winning the British Open Championship.

Being so honored in the Metropolitan Capital of the World—riding with the Honorable Mayor and Horton Smith, our president of the PGA, through the narrow, majestic canyons of concrete and steel as the thousands cheered block after block—the confetti of paper tape ribbons which darkened the sky—certainly gave me a thrill which I've never experienced before.

This most enthusiastic expression by this great multitude exemplified most explicitly how our patriotic citizens respect and honor the international success of their fellowman. And somehow I felt that the Royal and Ancient Sport, the game which I chose to pursue as a professional career, would take another step forward and the results of this grand reception would be for the best interest to golf.

(s) Ben Hogan

Ben Hogan's U. S. Open victory in 1950 is described by Des Sullivan, *Newark Evening News* (New Jersey). (Des, one of the best golfers of the Golf Writers Association of America, is now retired and lives in Myrtle Beach, South Carolina.) :

Many years have passed, but the recollection of 20 minutes late on the afternoon of June 10, 1950, remains as the most vivid moment in my career as a golf writer.

Seventeen months earlier, Ben Hogan's career—and life—apparently were ended in a fog-shrouded Texas highway smashup. Now the man who was never expected to walk again limped to the 72nd tee of the Merion Golf Club needing a par-4 on that 458-yard hole to tie for the U.S. Open championship. It was the first time since his accident that Hogan had walked 36 holes in one day, for him a physical torment that then was required by Open format. Although, characteristically, he denied that it bothered him, he obviously was in pain from a muscle he had wrenched in his left knee while driving on the 66th hole.

But the spirit overcame the weakness of flesh. He followed a 260-yard, into-the-wind, arrow-straight drive with a two-iron rifle shot that stubbornly refused to drift in toward the flagstick. It hit the green and pulled up 50 feet to the right of the hole.

Part of the tremendous crowd burst through the gallery lines for a better vantage point. I did not lead the charge through the bunker on the left side, but seconds later my chin was buried under the lip of the trap and my eyes peered anxiously through the grass on the fringe as Ben began his third stroke.

The ball agonizingly trickled five feet past. The next one curled in— and I couldn't cheer because my mouth was full of sand.

Hogan beat Mangrum and Fazio in a playoff the next day without the help of that historic two-iron. Someone had stolen it from his bag as he walked from the 72nd green to the clubhouse. But he had a better trophy.

Des Sullivan

20
Tony Jacklin

One of the finest chapters in the history of golf in Great Britain was recorded on the 12th day of July, 1969, when Anthony (Tony) Jacklin won the British Open championship. There was never a victory which meant more to the golfing pride of the British Empire. For 62 years the British dominated this title and they were actually the master golfers of the world for some 500 years. Then in 1922, Walter Hagen became the first American to break this reigning monopoly on the championship. Coincidental with this period, the United States achieved supremacy in golf and the great Empire that brought the game to the world silently stood aside. Henry Cotton, on three occasions, 1934, 1937 and 1947, won the Open, which salvaged some of the British pride. Then in 1951, when only a few of the international golfers participated, Max Faulkner became victorious. Apart from three scattered wins by the British, they were virtually out of contention.

In 1969 one Britisher rose from the depths of obscurity to the zenith of fame when he defeated the giant stalwarts of the game—Nicklaus, Player and others who had already achieved their fame. But their efforts were all in vain, because Jacklin commanded the rein of the oldest tournament in the game.

Yes—it was a Cinderella story when the youthful British Commoner, son of a truck driver, defeated the burly giants of the world to regain some glory to his native land. It was an impossible achievement, according to the prophesiers, that a golfer from the small British Isles could defeat the international immortals of the world. Although Tony's victory was astronomical, he was not considered a dark horse winner. To be sure, he had competed in four previous British Opens and in 1967, he came in fifth with a remarkable 285. His performance in the United States was a mark of excellence when he won the Jacksonville Open in 1968. It was, however, stated by one person that Tony happened to be in the right place at the right time and backed into the victory. Whatever that means. (This magazine did not advertise Tony's equipment.) This cast some doubt on Tony's ability. But this doubt was soon eliminated. It was inevitable that Tony would soon have the opportunity

Tony Jacklin barely misses a birdie putt on the 9th green of the National PGA Golf Course during the 3rd round of the 1971 National PGA Championship. Tony won both the British Open and the U.S. Open Championships within a one year period. (Photo by Nevin H. Gibson)

to prove himself. Less than one year later, the time arrived. It was the United States Open championship at the Hazeltine Golf Club, Chaska, Minnesota where 150 top professionals of the world were assembled to compete for this most prestigious title. The 7,151-yard course was rugged, contained many blind holes and, as alleged by Dave Hill, was not fit for play. Again, the odds were against Tony Jacklin. With the likes of Nicklaus, Player, Casper, Palmer and some 145 others, who would ever surmise that the dimunitive 5′ 9½″ youthful Englishman could possibly win this one?

In addition to this most difficult course, Mother Nature blew a 41-mph gale on the very first day of play. After the end of the round, the scoreboard read: Tony Jacklin—71. This was the only score in the field of 150 of the world's finest which was below par. Tony Jacklin was in front all the way and in the final round, he shot his third consecutive 70 to go with his opening 71 for a winning 281. His margin of victory was the greatest since 1921, when Jim Barnes won by nine strokes. Tony was once again in the right place at the right time, but he failed to back into the victory—he won it outright and most convincingly. He became the fourth man in history to hold both the British and the United States Open titles simultaneously. The big three, who played the same course and under the same conditions, were most thoroughly thrashed: Palmer by 24 strokes, Nicklaus by 23 and Player by 21. Tomorrow is another day, but on this 21st day of June, 1970, Sir Anthony (Tony) Jacklin reigned as the World's Greatest Golfer and her Majesty, the Queen of the British Empire who awarded Tony the OBE (Officer of the British Empire) in February, four months prior to this most outstanding triumph, blinked away a tear.

Tony Jacklin relates his greatest moment in golf:

I have had a number of great moments in golf but none would compare with that most exciting thrill which I experienced when I won the British Open Championship in 1969 at the famed Royal Lytham and St. Anne's Golf Course. The year before, when the Open was played at Carnoustie, I started with a pair of 72's for a 144 total which was four strokes behind Billy Casper, the leader at the time. Then I ended poorly with 75–80. I was most determined that I would not repeat this performance.

In the third round I scored my third consecutive sub-par score over the 6,826 yards of Irish Sea-swept links, and had visions of winning. The weather was most changeable, windy and overcast, then sunny and calm. I was paired with Bob Charles, the 1963 winner who was playing well apart from his third round. My 208 total was five under par. I felt no unusual tension, even after the 16th hole when I knew I was leading.

I never felt I had the tournament definitely won until we reached the final hole. Bob was on the green about 15 feet from the hole. I then hit my approach shot about 12 feet from the hole. When Bob's putt slid by, I knew I could three-putt and still be a winner. It was indeed a great feeling and of course the victory itself was my greatest moment in golf.

One of the contributing factors to my victory was my outstanding play with the sand wedge. The day before the Open, Roberto thought my old sand wedge was probably illegal as the grooves appeared too deep. I took it to the Royal and Ancient Committee and they said it was bordering illegal. I went to the Dunlop stand and took a new one off the rack. Of the eleven sand traps I was in during the championship, I successfully got up and down in two every time. I was honored with another great moment when her Majesty, Queen Elizabeth, awarded me the OBE (Officer of the British Empire) on her birthday in 1970.

Winning the U.S. Open was undoubtedly my greatest achievement in golf. The outstanding players of the world were participating and the competition was obviously much stronger than in the British Open. Also, winning by seven strokes is even hard for me to believe. In spite

Tony Jacklin tees off from the 12th tee of the Arizona Country Club during the second round of the 1971 Phoenix Open Championship. The famed "Camel Back" Mountain is seen in the background. (Photo by Nevin H. Gibson)

of the fact that I led all the way, I was under far more pressure than in the British Open. The constant thought of losing after retaining this lead was foremost in mind and it kept building up all the time as I progressed through each hole of play. I suppose in a way it prepared me better psychologically because I did manage to retain my composure to the finish. Winning—it was certainly great. One other important thing about this victory, it proved that my British Open victory was no fluke. It's always been my contention that the winners of major tournaments are the true champions, although at times some luck may play a part in the victory. Naturally, after I won the British Open I entertained some suspicious thoughts about luck but when I won the U.S. Open, this was all dissolved.

I suppose being British, and you chaps always winning our British Open, is perhaps one of the reasons why I select my victory of the British Open as my greatest moment in golf.

(s) Tony Jacklin

Dick Taylor, who provided Tony Lema's coverage for this volume, describes his introduction to Tony Jacklin:

After meeting Arnold Palmer, it was nearly one decade later when another meeting with impact was made. This time it was on the practice tee of the Yomiuri Country Club near Tokyo, prior to the World Cup competition.

Palmer was the object of the gasping fans as he banged out shots into the misty morning. Down at the other end of the tee in solitude was a young "unknown" diligently at work. He was swinging as few foreign players did at the time, from his toes.

One just had to desert Arnold Palmer for a glance at the young man. The inscription on his golf bag indicated the wiry fellow's name was Tony Jacklin. Veteran Peter Alliss arrived and introduced Tony as his partner in the event, representing England. Tony was on his honeymoon, one that took the couple around the world as he piled up experience which subsequently paid.

Alliss knows talent when he sees it and he advised that Jacklin should be watched in the future as he climbed his way up in international play. Tony proved to be pleasant, certain of his future and dedicated to becoming a star.

The second day the Englishmen were paired with Palmer and Jack Nicklaus, and prior to the tee off Tony was asked if he was nervous over the prospect. "Nervous? I can hardly wait to take a crack at the Yanks," he said without a trace of bravado. "I'll learn something, and also learn something about myself." And this has been a creed which finally took him into his first Masters where he was pitted with Palmer and the gallery had mistaken him for a foreign amateur player.

By day's end everyone who followed Palmer knew who Tony was, as he scored 70 to Palmer's 73 and was but one shot off the pace set after 36 holes by Bert Yancey. He subsequently finished in a tie for 17th, with Gay Brewer, the 1967 champion. Palmer was fourth.

But Jacklin was on his way. One year later he won the Greater Jacksonville Open championship. And in 1969, his zenith, he became the British Open champion. The 1970 USGA Open title was a rich frosting on his golfing cake.

21
Ruth Jessen

One of the most successful and certainly one of the most popular players ever to participate in the Ladies Professional Golf Association's tour is Ruth Jessen. The attractive tall (5′ 7″) blond had early ambitions to be a singer, but these interests were overshadowed by her devotion to excel in golf.

Ruth, a native of Seattle (also home to Pat Lesser, Anne Quast and Jo Anne Gunderson, all winners of major championships), won the Seattle City Championship three consecutive times: 1952, 1953, and 1954. She won the Pacific Northwest Championship in 1954 and 1955, and was the Washington State Champion in 1954. Miss Jessen, who also likes to swim and dance, attended Seattle University for one year and while there became one of the few women in history to earn a spot on the man's golf team.

Ruth turned professional in 1956 at the age of 19 and became the youngest professional on the women's tour. So impressive was her play that she became a member of the women's advisory staff for the Mac-Gregor Golf Company during her first year on tour. Starting with her victory of the Women's Tampa Open in 1959, through 1964, Ruth won eleven professional tournaments to become one of the top leading money winners and tournament winners. The increase in the prize purses of the LPGA during the decade of the 1960's enhanced a large number of top women amateurs to become professionals, increasing the competition on tour tremendously. Such names as Betsy Rawls, Mickey Wright, Kathy Whitworth, Carol Mann and a host of others, all great golfers, wrote another new chapter in the record book of the LPGA. Ruth, plagued with problems of consistent surgery for no less than five years during this period, made her record all the more incredible. Missing parts of 1962 and 1963, she still captured four victories within this period. Again in 1965, plagued with more surgery problems, she won the Haig and Haig Mixed Scotch Foursomes. Ruth missed a good portion of 1967 when she required further surgery to remove a rib in order to relieve a circulatory problem. In spite of these physical problems, Ruth maintained her status quo to retain her position in the

The attractive Ruth Jessen, one of the most popular professionals on the LPGA Tour, staged one of the finest comebacks of all times on February 21, 1971, by winning the richest tournament in the history of the LPGA. Plagued with continuous surgery over the years, Ruth returned to win the Sears Women's World Classic at the St. Lucie Country Club in Florida after a six-year strive for a victory. (Photo by MacGregor)

ranks of the top ten leaders. Through 1969, her all-time professional earnings were $119,287, placing her tenth among the leaders of the world.

Ruth tied for third place in the Lady Carling Open at Palmetto, Georgia, in 1969 while again recovering from surgery. This year, her greatest victory was her victory over cancer.

In 1971 Ruth won the Sears Women's World Classic, the richest golf tournament the LPGA has ever played, at St. Lucie Country Club, Florida. Ruth, still recovering from surgery and arriving on the scene with flu, rallied in the final round to defeat the largest field of competitors, 73, in the history of the LPGA, to win her first tournament since 1965. Ruth's rounds of 76–72–72—220 won by two strokes to give her a record purse of $10,000. More than 8,000 persons watched Ruth come from behind during the last round, not only defeating her competitors, but she won over a physical problem which had plagued her for years. It was incredible, stirring triumph. It was a miracle and comparable to those great victories Babe Zaharis and Ben Hogan achieved when they did the impossible. Ruth said after her great victory, "It was unreal."

Mary Ruth Jessen relates her four greatest moments in golf:

I guess there have been four great moments for me so far in my career, and all but one took place in 1964. The one was my first tournament win as a professional. At Tampa, Florida, (1959) at the Palma Ciea C.C. I had a ten shot lead with two holes to play, and it seemed like I tried my best to blow it. I made seven at the par three 17th and managed to scrape a par five out of the 18th hole. That was a cold winter in Florida, and I guess being a native of Seattle, Washington, helped me to win that first one.

In 1964, during the Dallas Civitan Open, I shot a 64 in the first round. I was thrilled, for this tied the world's record for women, which was held by Patty Berg at the time. The 18th hole at the Glen Lakes C.C. is a short, par-4, dog-legging left. Knowing I had to birdie that last hole to tie the record or hole it for two to break it, I took the short cut across the dog leg, leaving myself a short pitch shot to the green. I was able to hit that shot just as I wanted, landing about ten feet from the flag and rolling just past the pin about a foot. It was great fun shooting a 64 that afternoon.

The U.S. Women's Open was played at the San Diego C.C. that year. I had just finished my round, making a birdie on the last hole for a 292 total. Mickey Wright was playing behind me and needed a par to tie. This last hole was a long one, even for Mickey. She hit some kind of long iron for her second shot and caught the right-hand trap, but blasted out about six feet from the pin and holed it. My stomach finally returned to its normal place and again I knew I had another head to head match (I think) with the greatest of them all. Mickey had defeated me in 1962 in a playoff for the titleholders Championship, 70–72. Mickey again defeated me in this playoff 70–72. What was fun to me was that we both played good golf. There was only one bogey between us when Mickey three-putted the 9th. I do not know of any other Open Playoffs, men's or women's, with only one bogey in the round!

Omaha, Nebraska was the next one at the Miracle Hills C.C. Here I shot a record 200 for 54 holes on rounds of 69–67–64. The last putt I holed must have been 20 or 30 feet. This beat Kathy Whitworth out by one shot and again I had shot another round of 64. It's really difficut to say what is the most important, I guess they all are at the time. I would like to tell you this Mr. Gibson, without the help of the late Mr. Charles Congdon, who really taught me how to play the game, I might never had these great moments in golf. Chuck was the pro at the Tacoma Golf and Country Club, Tacoma, Washington.

(s) Mary Ruth Jessen

AUTHOR'S NOTE: It was also my good fortune to take my original golf lessons from the late Charlie Congdon when I was a member of his club from 1945 to 1950.

22
Bobby Jones

The time may come when some golfer may achieve the distinction by surpassing the phenomenal record established by the immortal amateur Robert Tyre Jones, Jr. Until that time arrives, Bobby Jones is the one and only to wear such a crown of glory.

With due respect to those immortal golfers who preceded and followed the era of Bobby Jones's reign, no one has yet reached the zenith which this immortal amateur achieved in major championship victories and his great "grand slam" of 1930.

It was in 1916 when Bobby Jones, then at the youthful age of 14, became a prominent name in golf by winning the Georgia State Amateur Championship. The eyes of the local citizens were focused on the youthful amateur, but then came the war, and golf, like many other things, was stymied for two years. After this, the amateur prodigy of Atlanta strived for five years and vied in eleven major events before winning his first major championship, which finally came in 1923. According to *A Pictorial History of Golf,* ". . . he defeated Bobby Cruickshank in a play-off for the U.S. Open Championship title." As Jones described it: ". . . we were all even on the last and decisive hole. I sliced to the short rough and the ball lay on the hard ground, clean . . . I suppose I had to decide again whether to play safe or go for it with an iron of about 200 yards. But I don't remember it. Stewart Maiden was near me. He told me later that I never played a shot more promptly or decisively. He says I picked a number two iron from the bag and banged it . . . I saw the ball on the green near the flag. Next thing I knew somebody was propping me up by the arm . . . I won the hole with a four to Bobby's six. And the Championship."

During the next seven years, Bobby entered 21 major events, won 13 and was runner-up in four. His thirteen major championship victories is an all-time world's record. Climaxing his most illustrious golfing career, in 1930 he won four major championships in a single year: the British Amateur, the British Open, the U.S. Open and the U.S. Amateur Championship (in that order). This incomparable achievement became renowned as the "Grand Slam."

One of the most prized photos in the author's collection, this picture illustrates Bobby Jones's most vivid expression of determination, concentration and fighting spirit, which are the requisites of winning. This photo was taken at Minneapolis on the 27th day of August, 1927, during the finals of the U.S. Amateur Championship when Bobby defeated "Chick" Evans to win his third U.S. Amateur title. (Photo willed to the author by the late David Scott Chisholm)

Bobby played on five U.S. Walker Cup teams in 1922, 1924, 1926, 1928 and 1930. He won all six of his individual singles matches and lost only one of his doubles.

The fabulous Walter Hagen was Bobby's contemporary. This most colorful professional won a total of eleven major titles from 1914 through 1929. Five of Hagen's major victories were the National PGA Championships in which Jones could not participate. By the same token, Jones won six amateur championships (majors) in which the Haig could not participate. During this period, Bobby Jones, the famous amateur, and Walter Hagen, the immortal professional, both distinctively different in many aspects except their goals in winning golf, made an immeasurable contribution to golf. Not only on the national level, but equally internationally as well. Both were tremendously popular in Great Britain and their victories "overthere" culminated a total of eight championships. During the era of these two immortals, other great names in sports came to the fore, such as Red Grange, the galloping ghost, Bill Tilden, Jack Dempsey, Gene Tunney, Johnny Weismuller, Earle Sande, Babe Ruth, Gene Sarazen, Paddock and even the horse "Man O'War" and this period of history became known as the "Sports Golden Decade."

The word golf and the name Bobby Jones were synonymous. However, it was not generally known that this most impeccable swinger played far less golf than his competitors. During the period when the "Emperor of Golf" was captivating the golfing world with his miraculous victories, among other things, he continued his studies at Georgia Tech in mechanical engineering, received a degree in English literature at Harvard, studied law at Emory University, taking the state bar examinations and passing them midway through his second year, then he quit to practice. As a result of these necessary curriculums, Jones averaged no more than three months per year of playing in championship competition. The presumption that he continually pursued the game is only natural by virtue of his amazing feats, but is a mythical assumption. This makes his most remarkable record even more incredible.

With reference to his thirteen major victories, which he achieved during a seven year period, and in view of the pace which the most awesome Jack Nicklaus is setting, it is now conceivable that this record is in jeopardy of duplication or even being surpassed. Now with the Masters Tournament added as a major event since its inception in 1934, an amateur could now possibly win five major championships in a single year. However, it is not conceivable that the "grand slam" will be surpassed.

Ben Hogan's three major victories in 1953 has thus far become the closest equivalent to the "grand slam's" achievement. Whether the "grand slam" will ever be excelled, or even duplicated—who knows? When, and if it should ever be, it will indeed become the greatest achievement in the history of golf.

At the age of 28, Bobby Jones climaxed his golfing career when he achieved that great grand slam in 1930. He immediately retired from competitive play after this most incomparable feat. The demands made upon Bobby by the sporting goods manufacturers, Hollywood's motion picture industries and publishers were most astronomical. Bobby was compelled by popular demand to disseminate his talents and knowledge of the game, which reached the golfing enthusiasts through various medias, including a series of motion pictures. His perfected swing, which was demonstrated in books, magazines, movies and in syndicated columns in newspapers, became the one and only method. Bobby's impeccable swing was the gospel. Bobby himself estimated that he wrote over a half million words on the subject of golf. Even today, some forty years later, a review of Bobby's films, articles and books shows the methods of swinging are basically the same as those taught by the present-day professionals.

During this same period, Bobby and some friends purchased 365 acres of land at a depression price in Augusta, Georgia, and formed the Augusta National Links, now the Augusta National Golf Club. The course, laid out with the assistance of Dr. Alister MacKenzie, became the venue for the Masters Tournament which commenced in 1934. It was inevitable that such a tournament, in which Bobby Jones was a part, would become successful. The Masters is now one of the four most prestigious championships. Mr. Bobby Jones and Mr. Clifford Roberts, the president and the tournament chairman respectively, operate the very best golf tournament in the world. Each year, some type of improvement is added to the grounds and facilities. The concessions provide excellent service at reasonable prices. Parking, golf programs, pairings and starting times, and checking services are free to the patrons. Most important, only the number of patrons which can be properly accommodated are admitted. Jack Nicklaus sums it up pretty well in his letter to the Masters: "As usual, the tournament was run with the dignity and perfection that will never be topped in the game of golf. I want to thank you both very much for allowing me to compete in this tournament. As I have said, Augusta National is my favorite golf tournament. I feel the Masters is a monument to everything great in golf."

The Masters Tournament is another most valuable contribution which Bobby Jones has made to golf. Perhaps, no other type of monument would be more appropriate to commemorate Bobby Jones than the Masters Tournament.

A crippling illness had made it impossible for Bobby Jones to play golf in the late 1940's. Bobby's health was then on the decline. Confined to a wheel chair, it was a real ordeal for him to make the annual trip to the Masters Tournament from Atlanta. I have not seen Bobby during the past two Masters Tournaments. Under these circumstances, I wrote his secretary in order to obtain his greatest moment in golf. At that time, even though Bobby could hardly sign his name, he responded:

I am completely unable to come up with any "Greatest Moment." For me, each tournament I played in was the most important thing in the world at the time, but faded back into proper perspective as soon as the finish had come. I wish you much success with your new book.

(s) Robert T. Jones, Jr.

23
Tony Lema

As told by Dick Taylor

Dick Taylor, editor of *Golf World* Magazine published in Southern Pines, North Carolina, first was golf editor of the Palm Beach, Florida, *Post-Times* and had South Florida as his beat. He has been with the weekly golf magazine since 1962 and has covered golf since 1948. Dick Taylor remembers the following about Tony Lema:

I remember Tony. Champagne Tony. Lema the lively. He afforded me the most memorable moment in golf when he won the 1964 British Open. When this young man, up from the caddie ranks, a possible candidate for delinquency at one time, strode up the 18th fairway of the old course on that brisk day in July, hackles rose on the neck.

When the huge gallery, restrained and courteous throughout the exciting week, burst from its confines and all but engulfed the Californian after his little pitch-and-run to the pin, the heart started pounding.

And when he tapped in a "tiddler" of a putt for victory, reached quickly into the cup, retrieved the ball and mightily flung it over the humanity-ringed green, tears welled in more than one observer's eyes. It was a great moment in golf in a great and historic setting, St. Andrews, Scotland.

He had gone out for his final round in a daze, fully aware that victory in this momentous classic was within his grasp. And when he passed the incoming Jack Nicklaus and realized the gifted Ohioan was charging the ancient links and was actually in the hunt, Tony shook off his nervous coma and produced some of the finest clutch golf ever seen.

He had 12 holes to go when Nicklaus finished with 68 and 284. What Tony did in response later led to an official of the sponsoring Royal and Ancient to describe the new champion as "one with a noble backbone." Quite so. For Lema's log over the final 12 holes eloquently speaks for itself: 333–334–443–443 for a closing 38–32 (70) and 279 total.

He had captured the lead after the second round and his composite was 73–68–68–70, the final two scores in a double round. Nicklaus had started poorly on 76–74, then magnificently carved from the ancient links 66–68 as closers, two rounds one day the likes of which had never before been performed.

Prior to the tee-off at the Cypress Point Golf Course during the 25th Annual Crosby Pro-amateur are (left to right) Tony Lema, Father John Durkin and Billy Casper. A few months later, Tony was killed in a tragic airplane crash near Chicago. (Photo by Bing Crosby)

For a golf writer, the assignment turned out to be a dream: on the same jet with Tony, living in the house next to where Tony and Doug Sanders stayed, and meeting with Fred Corcoran, Lema's business manager, when Tony wasn't available. It was something like living inside his head as he nightly ate at home, donned a black silk robe, quietly talked of the day, and retired early.

When he had gained the lead after the second round, despite an inability to regain regulation of time and sleeping habits due to the Atlantic crossing, he was all the more excited and admitted that he had actually gotten on his knees and prayed for help the final day. It was a victory he wanted badly.

And when finally in glory, he entered the press tent with its downhill lie and tea cups scattered over tables, the assembled cast of writers from all parts of the globe stood and gave him an ovation. He gave them champagne, of course, during the interview, amidst quaffs, and utter fatigue began to set in. His eyes were deep in their sockets, and his complexion ashen. The adrenals, pumping full bore since arrival, were shutting down.

His arrival had been somewhat bizarre. On the flight to Prestwick, Tony insisted that a few drams of Scotch make for a pleasing ocean crossing. He based this on a recent trip to Japan, where more than just a few drams are needed to get over the Pacific.

Protestations of a short flight were to no avail and doubles of smoked barley malt and conversation flowed for hours. A memorable fragment of the discussion centered on manager Corcoran's admonition to Lema that, "you should have left the Tour one week early and gone to Scotland. You'll never learn to play the Old Course in the time left." To which Tony replied, "I don't build courses, I play them and I'll play this one when I get to it."

To blow away the mists of time which have clouded Tony's preparation for the classic, he played 10 holes in his first practice session, 18 the next, then teed off in quest of the title the following day. At any rate, after several enjoyable hours of food and drink, Lema returned to the first cabin and had hardly learned the combination of coiling his body in comfort for a nap when the captain happily reported we would reach Scotland earlier than anticipated due to favorable tail winds.

And so it was, in diamond-bright daylight, that the small entourage stumbled off the airplane and into Scottish customs, where a prophesy was made. Sleepy-eyed Tony followed the line of disembarked visitors and came awake when one of the inspectors, a craggy-faced man of indeterminate age, asked, "it's Mr. MacLema, isn't it?" A foozled Tony corrected, "Lema, Tony Lema." And the canny Scot replied, "ach, noo, ye are the famous golfer come to Scotland to win the Open. So MacLema it is." This brightened the fatigued player considerably. And obviously struck its mark.

(s) dick taylor

24
Bob Murphy

Bob Murphy, the pudgy, Brooklyn-born, converted Floridian, made a most impressive showing in the ranks of professional golf during his very first year on the PGA Tour. He won his first victory, the Philadelphia Golf Classic, on the 25th day of September, 1968, after a sudden death play-off against Labron Harris and won the $20,000 first prize. One week later, he captured the rich Thunderbird Classic to win $30,000. The week prior to these successive victories, he tied for second place in the richest tournament of all, the Westchester Classic, to earn $20,416.66. Within a period of 18 days, Bob earned $70,416.66 and each shot he executed in play during this period was worth $85.78. By the end of the year, his official earnings of $105,595.00 placed him as the 10th leading money winner of the year. Bob's stocky physical stature, 5′ 10″ and 215 pounds, and his short, fast backswing, plus the fact that it was his first year on the Tour, makes his bid in the professional ranks even more incredible, if not miraculous.

In 1969, Bob suffered a slump during the second half because his clubs were stolen in Philadelphia, the venue of his first victory. He finally found a set in which he had confidence and his game improved again. He still earned $56,526.00 for the year and placed 32nd among the leading money winners.

Bob came back strong in 1970 and won the Hartford Open with rounds of 66–66–66–69 for a 267 total and seventeen under par to win by four strokes. A month earlier, Bob produced one of his finest single round performances in the prestigious National PGA Championship at Tulsa, Oklahoma. The course was the same on which he won the U.S. Amateur Championship in 1965, the Southern Hills Country Club. He was trailing the leader, Dave Stockton, by nine strokes and Arnold Palmer by four strokes at the end of three rounds. Then Bob shot a brilliant closing 66 to gain seven strokes on Stockton and four on Arnie which placed him in a tie with Arnold Palmer for second place. It was a most courageous endeavor which fell short by two strokes. Bob also placed second in the Coral Springs Open and the Tucson Open. He earned $120,639 for the year in official prize money

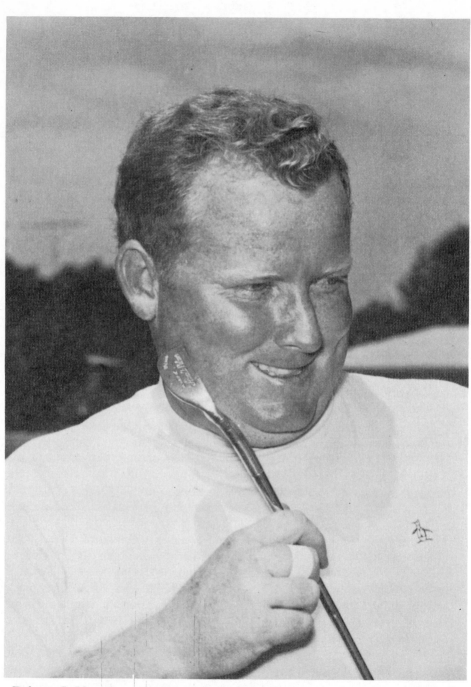

Robert J. Murphy, the dimpled, smiling Irishman, collected $70,416.66 in a three week period during his very first year on Tour. During this triumphal reign, Bob won two consecutive tournaments and was runner-up in the richest tournament of the year, the Westchester Classic. (Photo by Gene L. Scott)

Bob Murphy drives from the 5th tee of the National PGA Golf Course in Palm Beach Gardens during the third round of the National PGA Championship in 1971. Last year, Bob made a courageous effort to win this event at Tulsa when he finished with a blazing 66 to end as a runner-up with Arnold Palmer, two strokes behind the winner, Dave Stockton. (Photo by Nevin H. Gibson)

and was the ninth leading money winner for the year.

Early in 1971, although without an outright victory through April, Bob had earnings of $41,000. There is little doubt that he will not exceed the $100,000 mark as he has invariably played his best during the hot summer period. It was at humid Houston in 1969 when Bob opened with a 66 to lead the U.S. Open and he finished two strokes behind the winner.

Before turning professional and prior to his graduation from the University of Florida in 1967 with a degree in Physical Education, he won the 1965 United States Amateur Championship; 1965 and 1966 Florida Amateur titles; 1966 NCAA Championship; 1967 Florida Open; and was a member of the United States' World Amateur Team Championships squad in 1966 and the Walker Cup Team in 1967. Bob attended the University on a baseball scholarship, but he injured his shoulder in a pick up game of football during his freshman year and never did go out for the baseball team.

Robert J. Murphy, Jr., relates his greatest moment in golf:

My greatest moment would be winning the National Amateur in 1965, certainly my "coming of age" in golf. This was my first attempt in the U.S. Amateur and the first to be played entirely on a stroke basis. I was four strokes back after the first round and my second round of 69 put me in front by two strokes. Then on the third day, I scored a 76 which placed me in a tie with Bob Dickson and one stroke in front of Bill Campbell, the defending champion. During the last round, I shot a 73 for a 291 total and was in with the lead at this point. Bob Dickson played behind me and had earlier in the second round incurred a four stroke penalty, but when he reached the 70th hole, he had recovered from the penalty and held a one stroke lead. I just sweated it out. Unfortunately for Bob and lucky for me, he bogied the last two holes and I won by a single stroke.

(s) Bob Murphy

25
Jack Nicklaus

Within a very short period from this writing, it is most conceivable that Jack Nicklaus's achievements in golf will eclipse virtually all the golf records of the world and he will become renowned as the greatest golfer of all times. This is his ambition and the possibility of his chances to achieve this goal appears more probable at every major championship.

In 1956, Jack won the Ohio State Open title at the age of 16. During the next four years, he became the most talked-about amateur since Bobby Jones, winning no less than 13 significant amateur titles, including two U.S. Amateur Championships. Also, in 1960, he recorded the lowest score ever made by an amateur in the U.S. Open with rounds of 71–71–69–71 for a 282 to take second place.

Jack's decision to sacrifice his amateur status to become a professional became final when he decided to achieve his ambition to become the world's greatest golfer. Competing with the leading professionals for trophies in lieu of prize money would be the easier avenue to conquer this quest. Although the immortal Bobby Jones took this amateur route, the trend of golf had changed and it was inevitable that Jack would become a professional to compete on the same grounds and vie for the same money prize as the leading golfers. It was a challenge which Jack accepted.

Jack's debut in his very first professional venture, the Los Angeles Open in 1962, was not a sensational beginning. He finished at the very bottom of the money winners' list and earned the sum of $33.33. Unknown to many, Jack was quite ill during the tournament, but he finished. The descriptive tone of Jack's coverage in the sports page had changed to a tinge of doubt as to his ability to compete with the professionals. This doubt, if any really existed, faded rapidly.

Jack's first victory on the professional Tour was the most prestigious title of the world. He defeated the immortal Arnold Palmer in an 18-hole play-off to win the U.S. Open Championship at Oakmont, Pennsylvania, in 1962. Renowned as a powerful hitter who drives the ball prodigious distances, he won this event with the finesse of his

The powerful "Golden Bear" drives from the 5th tee on the 431-yard hole of the National PGA Golf Course in the third round of the National PGA Championship in 1971 at Palm Beach Gardens, Florida, en route to winning his second National PGA Championship. It marked Jack's 11th major title victory and he became the one and only to win all the four major titles on two occasions. (Photo by Nevin H. Gibson)

putter. Jack mastered Oakmont's fast and tricky greens and only three-putted once over 90 holes while Arnie three-putted eight. From that moment on, he shared the limelight, if not the popularity, with Arnold Palmer.

At this time, Arnie had captured the admiration of the gallery. He was the sentimental favorite in every tournament he entered. He was the one and only to many. His magnetic personality, combined with the most fabulous record of major victories which he amassed over a relatively short period, attracted millions into "Arnie's Army." His courageous style of play and his vivid expressions were also factors which favored his popularity.

Jack was just beginning. Within a short period, his performance of play and habit of winning practically every major event demanded attention and Jack soon attracted a group called "Jack's Pack" who followed the "Golden Bear."

Since becoming a pro, this awesome golfer has now won nine major championships. He is the only player to win every major title of the world at least twice. Jack admittedly points toward winning the major championships: the U.S. Open, the PGA Championship, the British Open and the Masters. "The accomplishment that would separate me from other golfers," said Jack, "is to win more major championships. That would be a quality achievement. I always aim for the four majors. Winning one is a condition for getting into the World Series of Golf. Then if you can beat the other three guys who have won a major championship, well I feel like you've proven something. It gives me a great feeling and a great deal of personal satisfaction when I accomplish this."

Jack Nicklaus hits an approach to the 5th green during the dramatic play-off against Lee Trevino for the 1971 U.S. Open Championship at the famed Merion Golf Course in Oakmont, Pennsylvania. At least 10,000 spectators witnessed this exciting match which Lee Trevino won with his 68 to Jack's 71. (Photo by Nevin H. Gibson)

Jack Nicklaus putting on the 11th green en route to winning the Walt Disney World Open in December 1971 during a Florida mist. This victory boosted Jack's earnings for the year to a record $244,490.50. At this writing Jack is now the all-time leading money winner. (Photo by Nevin H. Gibson)

Jack Nicklaus makes a complete follow through from the 4th tee of the par-3 235-yard hole at the Whitemarsh Valley Country Club during the 1971 Philadelphia Golf Classic. (Photo by Nevin H. Gibson)

The "Golden Bear" expresses determination during the 1971 Philadelphia Golf Classic. (Photo by Nevin H. Gibson)

The prodigious Jack Nicklaus putting on the final hole during the 1971 Masters Tournament. A three time winner of this prestigious event, Jack came in second here. (Photo by Nevin H. Gibson)

Jack has experienced this personal satisfaction by winning the World Series of Golf on four occasions out of seven efforts. The three times he failed were in 1965, 1966 and 1971 when he was the runner-up. In 1966 he lost in a sudden death play-off to Gene Littler. This incredible performance surpasses the records of all the other participants combined.

Jack exceeded the million dollar mark in official earnings some time ago. He has on four occasions been the "Leading Money Winner of the Year." He was second on three occasions and twice he was third. His worst effort in this department was in 1970 when he was fourth and only won $140,167. In 1971 he won a record of $244,490.50.

The "Golden Bear" started early in 1972 by winning the Bing Crosby National Pro-Am after defeating the youthful John Miller in a sudden death play-off. Within weeks, he came in second in the richest event of the year, Jackie Gleason's Inverrary Classic. This effort elevated his career earnings to $1,477,286 which by-passed Arnold Palmer and he reached another milestone as be became the all-time leading money winner of the world.

One of the greatest golf stories of our times is Jack's book, *The Greatest Game of All: My Life in Golf,* in which he collaborated with Herbert Warren Wind. Here we have the greatest golfer and writer combining their talents in this classic treatise. It gives an outstanding account of Jack's life and his greatest achievements in golf.

Jack Nicklaus relates his greatest moments in golf:

My greatest moment in golf was winning my first U.S. Open Championship which was actually my first professional tournament victory. This was in 1962 at the Oakmont Country Club near Pittsburgh. After the second round I trailed Arnold Palmer and Bob Rosburg by three strokes. I was paired with Billy Maxwell for the final 36 holes which at that time were played on the third day. After the third round, Arnold Palmer and Bobby Nichols were leading me by two strokes. Bob had a 73 and I played the last 12 holes in three under par to score a 69 while Arnie had a 71 and we were tied for the lead at 283. In the play-off, my putter stayed hot and I scored a 71 while Arnie had a 74. This first victory, compounded by the fact that I defeated Arnie in the playoff, was naturally a great feeling and my greatest moment in golf.

Another great moment was in 1965 when I established a record 271 to win my second Masters title. Although I won it again the following year to become the first to successfully defend this title, defeating Ben Hogan's record by three strokes was something else. After two rounds, "The Big Three" which we were called, that's Palmer, Player and myself, were tied for the lead. Then I scored a 64 to tie the record which Lloyd Mangrum established 25 years earlier and I led Player by five strokes and Arnie by eight. My closing 69 gave me the title by nine strokes which was the largest margin of victory in the history of the Masters. When I won it the first time, I though that it would be the biggest thrill I would ever have. However, my win this time, and the manner in which I won has surpassed all my thrills in golf. Augusta National is my favorite course and the Masters is my favorite golf tournament. I feel the Masters is a monument to everything great in golf.

My next greatest moment came in 1967 at the Baltusrol Golf Club's Tower course, in Springfield, New Jersey, when I established a new record of 275 to win my second U.S. Open title. I played with Arnold Palmer during the final round and we were tied with Billy Casper, the defending champion, one stroke behind Marty Fleckman, the leader. Palmer went ahead of me at the second hole, but I caught him with a birdie at the third and I was never behind again. Casper scored a 72 while Marty faded to an 80. Beginning with the third hole, I birdied five of the next six and scored a 31 on the front side and was then four strokes ahead of Arnie. A bogey five on the 10th and birdies on the 13th and 14th, left me needing one more birdie to break the record which Ben Hogan established in 1948. I was scared. The par-5 18th hole was my chance. My tee shot was off to the right in the rough. I was forced to play safe short of the water on my second and now only a miracle would give me a birdie which I needed for the record. I had the tournament practically cinched at this point, but at this precise moment, I was definitely annoyed after missing a good chance for a birdie and a possible record. I decided on a hard one iron and hit the best long iron I've ever hit to the front right side of the green, 22 feet from the hole. With the recently acquired white-headed putter, I dropped the putt for a record 275 and won by five strokes.

(s) Jack Nicklaus

26
Arnold Palmer

It was at the Eastern Open in Baltimore during the latter 1950's before Arnold Palmer became an immortal golfer when I first saw him hit a golf ball. On his second shot on a par-5 hole at the Mt. Pleasant Golf Course, he asked his caddy if he could reach the green. The caddy observed the tight fairway lie, then replied, "No, because you can't hit a wood from that lie." Arnold looked at the distant green, hesitated momentarily, tugged at the waist of his trousers, then grabbed an iron from the bag, a one or a two, and plowed through the shot. The ball carried the green, which astounded me, and the embarrassed caddy sighed, "Gee Whiz." Arnie expressed a grimace in the tone of "I thought I could," handed the club to the caddy, hitched up his trousers, raised his head high and marched toward the green, looking to the right and then to the left. This characteristic in Arnie's play has never ceased and he attracts an army of followers at every venue he plays, whether he is in contention for the lead or otherwise.

Apart from Arnold's 1954 U.S. Amateur victory and his two British Opens, I've seen him win every major title and some sixteen other PGA events. However, I shall never forget that very first shot I saw him execute which left me with a most vivid impression of his exciting style of performance.

"Doc" Giffin, former PGA Press Secretary and now Arnold Palmer's assistant, describes one of Arnold's greatest moments in golf:

When one is privileged, as I have been, to have worked closely with and later for Arnold Palmer during most of his and the game's magnificent decade of the 1960s and tries to single out Arnold's greatest moment, he faces an impossibility. Too many of Palmer's achievements qualify for that label: the 1960 Open, when he made up seven strokes in the last round; the Masters that same year, when he birdied the last two holes for victory; in fact, each of his victories in the major championships and many others of the 70-plus tournaments he has won could be classed as a great moment.

The 1962 Masters stands out in my mind for two reasons: it so typified the "Hairbreadth Harry, "don't-ever-count-me-out" style of Arnold Palmer which has captivated golf fans everywhere and it was my first "working" Masters.

Arnold Palmer, the immortal professional, drives during an exhibition match for the U.S. Air Force. This drive, snapped just prior to impact, carried the ball some 310 yards down the center of the narrow fairway. Note the muscular "blacksmith" left arm which must play some part in the fact that Arnie drives the ball such prodigious distances. (Photo by U.S. Air Force)

Just the year before at Augusta National, Arnold had left the golfing world in a state of shock when, with the opportunity to become the first back-to-back Masters champion only a hole away, he double-bogeyed the 72nd and turned the title over to Gary Player. Similar ingredients for defeat turned up in the late stages of the 1962 Masters, but Arnold has never been an "Oh, here we go again" guy. Twice—in the final round and in the ensuing playoff—he dug himself out of the hole to stay alive and then won after losing the lead he had held through the two middle rounds.

With memories of the crushing defeat of 1961 still in his mind and rehashed constantly by the huge Master's press corps in the days before the tournament, Arnold set out resolutely to obliterate it all. He followed up a steady opening-round 70 with his lowest Masters score—a 66—to take a two-stroke lead at the halfway point.

Arnold Palmer expresses his emotions most vividly in his characteristic finish. Arnie is approaching the 13th green during the third round of the 1970 National PGA Championship at Tulsa. His efforts were in vain, as it marked the third time the immortal professional has come in second in the only major event he has failed to capture. (Photo by Nevin H. Gibson)

He almost birdied in from 13, running off four in a row before missing from just eight feet at the 17th for a fifth in a row.

A 69 Saturday maintained his two-stroke lead, now over his old tour pal and occasional traveling companion, Dow Finsterwald. Player was third, but four strokes behind him. Other than Gene Littler, who eventually finished two strokes off the pace, nobody else had a chance on the demanding Augusta National course.

The drama built early. Arnold and Gary were paired together, playing behind Dow. None of the three started auspiciously, particularly Arnold. Those of us who knew something about Arnold's feelings about scoring on Augusta National had an inkling that Arnold was not sharp when he missed an 18-inch birdie putt on the par-five second hole. (Arnold maintains that the second hole must be birdied to do well on the front nine.) Gary also failed to make a four there, but birdied four other front-nine holes to fashion a 35 going out. With nary a birdie and three bogeys on that nine, Arnold fell into a tie with Gary at the turn. A struggling Finsterwald was just a stroke behind.

Then, to compound his troubles, Arnold double-bogeyed the lovely 10th hole. When Palmer and Player reached the par-three 16th, the situation appeared dangerous for Gary and almost hopeless for

Arnold, particularly when he put his five-iron tee shot just off the back edge of the sloping green. In comparison to Finsterwald's score through 15 holes, Gary trailed by a stroke and Arnold by three.

Then came one of the most remarkable shots of the brilliant Palmer career. Wedging down the grade from 50 feet, he put the ball into the cup for a birdie. Exclaimed fellow pro Bob Rosburg, watching the shot on television in the clubhouse: "He stared that ball into the hole." Gary missed a nine-foot birdie putt after the uproar subsided. Up ahead, Finsterwald had bogeyed the 17th and finished with a 73. With the usual cordon of Pinkerton and green-coated Masters officials, he had gone to Clifford Roberts' quarters in the clubhouse to wait and watch on TV.

Fired by the remarkable shot at 16, Arnold arched his approach 15 feet from the cup at 17 and ran in the birdie putt. Player parred and the two went to the 18th tee needing pars to tie Finsterwald. They got them, Gary routinely and Arnold from 30 feet above the hole on the tricky green.

In the Monday play-off, Arnold again experienced front-nine birdie famine, Dow fell out of contention early and Gary seized quick command with birdies on the first two holes. At the turn, he was three strokes in the lead.

Arnold Palmer drives from the 10th tee of the Augusta National Golf Course during the third round of the 1971 Masters Tournament. This all-time leading money winner was the first and, at this writing, the only one to capture this prestigious title on four occasions. (Photo by Nevin H. Gibson)

This day, though, the pivotal hole for Arnold was to be the 10th, which sweeps down a slope to a semi-elevated green nestled among the pines and a magnificent variety of flowering plants and shrubs. Gary was long with his approach and the ball trickled down the embankment behind the green. He missed a six-foot putt for a bogey after Arnold ran in a 30-foot birdie putt. Two holes later, on the treacherous, par-three 12th, Arnold birdied again from four feet after a perfect eight-iron tee shot. Gary three-putted from 50 feet and Arnold was back in front.

He picked up three more strokes with birdies on the next two holes to Gary's par-bogey and coasted home with a three-shot victory, his most important in a nine-win season in which "charge" became a golf term synonymous with Palmer and his reputation as one of the game's all-time greats became firmly established.

Dick Taylor, the *Golf World* Magazine editor who contributed the Tony Lema article, describes his introduction to Arnold Palmer:

During the 1950s one of the innumerable fund-raising committees in Palm Beach County was putting together a winter benefit exhibition match at Tequesta Country Club where Dow Finsterwald was then the pro as well as a tour star. The four principals had been selected, but one player had to cancel and Dow suggested as a replacement the new Canadian Open champion, Arnold Palmer, his house guest. "And do you know what they told me?" asked Dow. "The sponsors said they wanted another 'name' to insure success. I told them they were about to pass up the next super star in professional golf and no one believed me."

Knowing that "Finsty" was a good judge of golf flesh we sought out this young man. The conversation while leaning on a counter in the golf shop is forgotten, but not the impression. In show business they call it "presence," and this man had it. He was a combination of halfback and middle-weight with the mien of a leader. And none of the qualities were offensive, for he had a big plus on his side: he obviously liked people.

The day of the exhibition arrived and a fair-sized gallery attended. But the fans missed the real show up front on the course in the form of Palmer in a quartet of good players, obviously playing a nassau. We deserted the charity match when they strode by on an opposite fairway and watched several holes. And this provided a great moment in golf-watching. Palmer was playing, with great relish, as if the U.S. Open title were at stake, bombing the tight course as no one ever had before. His companions were in pleasurable shock as Arnie disregarded obvious topographical road signs which pointed the way to playing the hole in par.

The incident at the time was not recognized as a great moment, although it proved memorable. But as the years fled by, that first meeting and subsequent peek on course have grown in the mind's eye. And it is to Palmer's credit that he has changed little since that time despite his success, adulation and harrassment. The same impact remains, the full-bore style remains, and his personality has attracted an army for him to lead.

27
Johnny Pott

Before becoming a professional in 1956, Johnny Pott was the number one man of the Louisiana State Golf Team which won the NCAA Championship. A native of Missouri, the 6' 1", 185 pounder came very close in two events before he was able to capture his first PGA Tour victory. At the Chicago Open in 1959, he held a nine stroke lead over Ken Venturi after the second round. He finished with 72–72 while Ken shot 68–66 to gain ten strokes and the victory by one stroke. Again in January of 1960 at the San Diego Open after three rounds of play, he led Mike Souchak by one stroke and finished with a fine 69, but Mike's 67 defeated him by a stroke.

Johnny's first Tour victory came on September 5, 1960, at the Dallas Open where he defeated Ted Kroll and Bo Wininger in a sudden death play-off.

Ironically, before Johnny won his second victory, he was also a runner-up on two occasions. This all happened in a three week period during three successive tournaments. On November 20, 1960, he was a runner-up to Lionel Hebert in the Cajun Classic Open and during the following week, he was a runner-up to Arnold Palmer when Arnie scorched the course with a last round 65 to win the Mobile Open. But after ending as a runner-up during two successive weeks, he captured his second PGA Tour victory the following week by winning the West Palm Beach Open on December 4, 1960.

In 1962, he won the Waco Turner Open and in the following year, he captured the American Golf Classic at Akron, Ohio, which was one of his finest tournament achievements. Over the monster Firestone course, his total 276 was four strokes in front of the runner-up, Arnold Palmer, who had robbed him of the Mobile title.

Johnny was a member of the PGA Tournament Committee from 1963 to 1965. He was also a member of the United States Ryder Cup team in 1963, 1965 and 1967.

During the decade of the 1960s, his "Tournament Play Stroke Average" was 71.590 per round. He won five PGA tournaments, was runner-up sixteen times, and on seven occasions, he finished third.

The smiling Johnny Pott, winner of the 1962 American Golf Classic over the monster Firestone Golf Course in Akron, Ohio. His 276 was four strokes in front of the runner-up, Arnold Palmer. Johnny was a member of the U.S. Ryder Cup team on three occasions: 1963, 1965 and 1967. (Photo by Spalding)

During this period, Johnny won $342,804.22 in official PGA earnings.

Johnny's fifth Tour victory was his most thrilling, the Bing Crosby National in 1968 which he had to win by the play-off route and he describes this action in his narrative. Just recently, he won the Gulf States PGA Section Championship and therefore qualified for the National PGA Championship of 1971.

Johnny Pott relates his greatest moments in golf:

Golf is a very exciting game. I have had many thrills, some winning, some disappointments and some other accomplishments.

My greatest thrill was winning my first tournament at Dallas in 1960. Next, winning the same year at West Palm Beach. This second thrill was wondering if I would ever win another tournament and making sure the first one wasn't luck. I have won a few others since then.

Making the Ryder Cup Team three times was my biggest achievement. Representing the United States is exciting enough. I was Arnold Palmer's partner in the first match I played in 1963. We had the option of playing the smaller British ball or our American ball. He asked me which ball I was going to play and I said the biggest one around. This is a most pressure-packed event and playing for the possession of that gold cup is a lot of pressure.

My most exciting win was the 1968 Bing Crosby National. I was in a sudden death play-off with Billy Casper and Bruce Devlin and when I missed the green with my approach shot, my chances of surviving this first extra hole appeared very dim at this point. Then I executed a fine chip shot and the ball actually rolled into the hole. The gallery screamed. The tournament was televised nationwide and I have never hit a shot seen by so many and talked about so much.

(s) Johnny Pott

28
Dave Ragan

Dave Ragan, Jr., became a professional in 1956. He won his first professional tournament in 1959, when at the youthful age of 23, he captured the Eastern Open Championship. From that year until 1962 he failed to win a tournament but placed second seven times, although his official earnings exceeded $50,000. A 41-month victory drought ended when Dave won the Beaumont Open and a month later, he captured the West Palm Beach Open in his native state after defeating Doug Sanders in a sudden death play-off. These victories enabled him to qualify for a berth on the United States Ryder Cup Team.

It was on a hot afternoon on July 21, 1963, at Dallas, Texas, when Dave came close to winning his first major championship but a rookie professional by the name of Jack Nicklaus was hotter than the weather and made a sensational finish, and Dave became a runner-up in the National Professional Golfers Championship.

Before turning professional, Dave Ragan, the son of a dentist, won the Florida high school title, the Florida Open and the Southern Inter-Collegiate Championship while at the University of Florida. The friendly muscular blond is a strong advocate of Christian life and Dave is highly respected by his fellow professionals and his followers.

Dave Ragan relates his greatest moment in golf:

I think that the greatest honor that I have had in golf was realized when I was selected to play for the United States on the 1963 Ryder Cup Team. Out of this honor came one of my most exciting moments.

Billy Casper and I were drawn to play Peter Allis and Christy O'Conner in one of the first round matches which was a two ball—alternate shots. We struggled all morning long, but Bill and I somehow managed to be three up going to the 15th which we lost when Billy just missed a tough, short putt for a birdie-4. Then on the 16th, Bill hit a great long iron that just missed going into the hole, but kept rolling and ended up about six feet over the green in the tough, wiry Bermuda grass. I hit a poor chip about 12 feet by and Bill just couldn't get that one down. We were then one up going into 17 which we managed to halve when I hit the hole with a chip shot that stopped

Dave Ragan, the likeable blond Floridian, was a member of the Ryder Cup team in 1963, from which derived his greatest moment in golf. During the same year, he fired a final 69 in the National PGA Championship at Dallas, but some "rookie," Jack Nicklaus, closed with a 68 to win. (Photo by Spalding)

just inches away. Christy and Peter had the honor on the 18th, a par three about 235 yards long. By the time we got to the 18th tee, the other three matches were either halved or lost, so there was a lot riding on this last hole. Peter hit a great wood shot that stopped about nine feet from the hole. Bill and I were pretty sick when we saw that shot, but somehow I managed to hit a one iron about 35 feet to the left of the hole. The putt I left Bill was an awfully tough putt that broke about three feet over a hump in the middle back of the green. As I finished giving my partner a weak word of "knock it in," I walked over to Dick Forrester, a PGA vice president who was also our match official, and said that of all the people that could be putting this important putt, I was glad it was Casper. About that time, and I really didn't want to look, I heard him tap the ball. Since Billy is one of the greatest lag putters in the business, I was shocked to see the ball slide about eight feet past the hole even though the greens were very slick. I was just numb. There is something about playing for others that sometimes tightens you up more than when you are playing for your own score. Christy putted next and missed his putt, which I am sure he wanted to make as badly as I wanted mine. As I stood over that 8-footer, which looked like 25 feet, words just couldn't express how much I wanted it to go in. How it got in, I just don't know. I'm sure it was only by the grace of God. As a result, we won the first point in the 1963 Ryder Cup matches, 1-up. That was really a great moment for me.

I have been fortunate enough to win some tournaments on the tour and they, too, were great moments for me in golf, especially my first win, the 1959 Eastern Open at Baltimore. Another great moment was when I won the 1963 Senior Service Championship in Scotland, which was the largest money tournament ever held in Europe at that time. I have won quite a bit of money in my life, many trophies and have received a certain measure of fame in golf. But you know, it doesn't take long for those trophies to tarnish and it doesn't take long to spend all the money you win and it certainly doesn't take long for people to forget who you are or who you think you are. So if I were to tell you about the greatest moment in my life it would not be about golf. It would have to be when I asked Jesus Christ to come into my life as my Lord and Saviour. He has never left or forsaken me. He has met my every need and He has never disappointed me. I'm sure it would sound silly to say I have no problems. I do and so does everyone else, but I've found that if I put my trust in Christ and keep my eyes on Him, He shows me how to walk on top of my problems.

(s) Dave Ragan

29
*Chi Chi Rodriguez**

* The author gives due credit to the book *Little Men in Sports* by Larry Fox, from which most of Chi Chi's coverage was obtained.

"I won't say anything . . . ," a suddenly serious Rodriguez began. "This is the first tournament I've ever won and I won't say anything until the man who is my second father, the man who made me into a golfer, Mr. Ed Dudley, is here beside me." This was the first day of September 1963. Summer had not quite left the Rocky Mountains of Colorado, but white peaks ringing the horizons of the Denver Country Club, the venue for the Denver Open, gave promise of cold weather to come. Now it was late afternoon and the tournament had ended. Juan (Chi Chi) Rodriguez of Puerto Rico, 5 feet, 7½ inches tall and a wiry 119 pounds, had roared from behind on the final round to win the title. Club officials presented Chi Chi with his winning check for $5,300, fitted him into the champion's winning jacket—they had to scramble to find one his size—and then asked the twenty-seven-year old golfer to say a few words.

The ceremony resumed when Ed Dudley arrived. Chi Chi wasn't the first youngster Dudley had helped. His pupils had even included Bing Crosby, Bob Hope, and President Eisenhower. But this was the first time he'd been so publicly recognized. "I'm very proud of Chi Chi," said Dudley, his 6 feet, 4 inches and 200 pounds dwarfing the young champion. "I never thought anybody would give me credit like this— for something I was proud to do." And then the short, olive-skinned Juan Rodriguez and the tall, white-haired Ed Dudley began to cry in each other's arms.

Dudley had been the golf professional at Dorado Beach Country Club in Puerto Rico when Rodriguez got out of the Army six years earlier. He took a youngster who had been working for $80 a month as an orderly in a psychiatric clinic and made him into a tournament golfer who had just earned $5,300 for four days' work. Dudley had long since left Dorado Beach and was the head professional at the Broadmoor Club in Colorado Springs. He was sixty-three years old and not in good health. His protege's final and winning round was the last

The diminutive Chi Chi Rodriguez, only 5' 7½" and 119 pounds, a happy-go-lucky native of Puerto Rico, drives the ball farther than most touring professionals. Chi-Chi, referred to as the "clown of the links," is one of the gallery's most popular professionals. His ability to joke with the group and then settle down and concentrate is most amazing. (Photo by Spalding)

he'd live to see. Aware that Chi Chi was in contention and going into the final day's play, Dudley traveled the 60 miles to Denver and gave his old pupil a putting lesson. Juan didn't really need any help with his putting, but he did need a friend in his corner. Dudley walked the final nine holes with Chi Chi, mentally boosting him to the championship in that pressurized final drive. Two months after the tournament, Ed Dudley died of a heart attack.

Earlier, when Ed Dudley left Dorado Beach, he was replaced by Pete Cooper, a professional who played and won often on the circuit, particularly in Florida on the Bermuda grass courses. Juan thought he was pretty good by this time. "I bet I could play on the tour, too," he told Cooper. "Not until you start beating me," his new boss replied—

Chi Chi Rodriguez expresses his elations with a little dance, a characteristic in his play, when a tricky putt dropped during the 1970 Masters Tournament on the ninth green of the Augusta National Golf Course. (Photo by Nevin H. Gibson)

The diminutive (5′ 7½″, 119 pounds) Chi Chi Rodriguez drives from the 14th tee during the 1971 U.S. Open Championship at the Merion Country Club at Oakmont, Pennsylvania. His playing partner, "Big George" Archer, is the tallest player on the Tour. (Photo by Nevin H. Gibson)

and soon Juan was indeed beating Pete Cooper. The next time Cooper was ready to leave on the tour, he lived up to his word. Without warning, he told Juan one day, "Well, let's go. You can live with me on the road." And so it was in 1960—Chi Chi played in twelve tournaments, finished fourth once, and earned $2,200. In 1961, he doubled his appearances, but earned no more money. He was so little, in fact, he played with women's clubs until 1962, when he switched to the smallest size made for men. The year of the switch, he earned $6,300, but the following year he finally began to make a name for himself and won $18,000.

Chi Chi won the Lucky International and the Western Open the next year. In 1967, he won the Texas Open and in 1968, the Sahara Invitational. Today, Chi Chi can earn $50,000 from tournament winnings alone. Exhibitions, endorsements, and fees for lessons may easily triple that. He also holds the prestigious position of the head pro at the Dorado Beach Country Club. This is where it all began, and Chi Chi is the first native islander to be given such a job, thanks to Ed Dudley who broke down the first barriers.

Chi Chi relates his greatest moment in golf:

You know, Mr. Gibson, I have had many great moments in golf and it's funny, one supersedes another. Back in 1962 when I tied for third place in the Dallas Open, this was my greatest moment at the time, then winning the Denver Open as my first victory on the PGA Tour was my greatest. I'm sure my victory in the prestigious Western Open Championship was my greatest achievement in golf and was also a great moment. But you know when I look back and review them all, I must say, actually winning a championship was not my greatest moment. It was, in fact, after winning, which I'm sure will always be my greatest moment in golf.

Mr. Ed Dudley was the one who started me and gave me the first real opportunity in golf. He lived a full life, loved everyone, had no enemies and was easy-going, just like his great golf swing back in 1931 when he won the Western Open. Well, Mr. Dudley was in bad health and he still came up from Colorado Springs to see me finish in the Denver Open. His presence inspired me to some extent to win my first championship. The victory itself was really not my greatest moment, although it was derived from it. But during the ceremony, when Mr. Dudley put his arms around me and we were both crying—this was indeed my greatest moment in golf. And I'm sure it shall never be superseded.

30
Barbara Romack

With her beauty and magnetic personality, not to mention her wit and intellectual knowledge, Barbara Romack could have succeeded in any profession she choose. However, these qualities do not necessarily lend themselves to playing competitive golf. To be sure, they are advantageous factors and golf is about 100% psychological and Barbara's qualitative qualifications would blend in well to meet this requirement. Without further ado on Barbara's build-up, she did indeed become a professional golfer after a most successful venture into the amateur ranks and, needless to say, she did succeed.

Barbara is a special member of the Brunswick Corporation's Consumer Division and Public Relations staff, promoting sports to women. Barbara does as much for the game of golf off the links as she does on. She is a past president of the LPGA and has served the LPGA during most of her professional career. Not only has Barbara served golf through her executive functions, but she has enhanced the image of golf, bringing many women into the sport. Barbara holds the all-time scoring record on Shell's Wonderful World of Golf, a fantastic 65.

Barbara first appeared on the national golf scene in 1952 when she won the California State Amateur Crown, the South Atlantic Championship, and the North and South title. She added the Canadian Amateur title to her collection in 1953, and then won her biggest victory in 1954, the U.S.G.A. Women's Amateur. Other amateur championships which Barbara won were: the Byron Nelson Junior Girls, Sacramento City Championship, Northern California Girls Junior, Indio Invitational, Pebble Beach, Valley Open (3 times), and she was the semi-finalist in the Texas Open, losing to Babe Zaharis in extra holes. Her greatest thrill in this event was when she defeated the immortal Betty Jameson on the 25th hole and Marlene Bauer, 2-up. After the match, she met her idol, Ben Hogan. Continuance of her victories: Ormand Beach (three times), California State (four times), Northern California, Thunderbird Invitation, runner-up in the British Women's Amateur, winner Palm Beach, St. Augustine (two times), Low Amateur Tampa Open and, as mentioned, the U.S. Women's Ama-

Barbara Romack, past president of the LPGA, holds the all-time record on Shell's Wonderful World of Golf, a fantastic 65. Prior to turning professional, Barbara defeated Mickey Wright in the finals of the U.S. Women's Amateur Championship in one of the most dramatic finishes in the history of the event. From this, Barbara received her greatest moment in golf. (Photo by MacGregor)

teur Championship. In the latter event, according to Barbara, "were the finest hours in my life." Further, she states: "The parade and welcome given by the people of the old Hometown was one of the greatest moments of my career." Also, "I'll always remember the awesome occasion of lunching with President Eisenhower at the White House."

Barbara Romack quotes her greatest moment in golf:

You ask me to tell you about my greatest moment in golf . . . and that is one tough question!! When you've been coached by Tom LoPresti, Ben Hogan, Byron Nelson and the late, great Tommy Armour; played with Jack Nicklaus, Sam Snead, Lloyd Mangrum, Ken Venturi, the late Dwight D. Eisenhower, Bob Hope, Bing Crosby, Phil Harris and Jackie Gleason; won the championships of two countries—the United States and Canada—and gone to the finals of the British Amateur; defeated Arnold Palmer and Dow Finsterwald on CBS Sports Spectacular with partner Mickey Wright; and shot a 65 on Shell's Wonderful World of Golf, you've had a lot of great moments. Winning a tournament, having a sensational scoring round, hitting an important shot or sinking a putt at the RIGHT *time during a match or round, and sometimes even a loss can be a great moment.*

There is, however, one particular moment that stands out in my mind so vividly. It was a win! The Women's National Amateur Championship in 1954. This is the ultimate goal in amateur golf and a goal I had set for myself at a very early stage of my career. The achievement of such has had a tremendous impact and influenced my career and life greatly. During the championship, I played the most consistent golf of my life. It was the "one time" that everything fell into place. Although I was shooting sub-par golf in every match, I was not picked as one of the favorites to win, as I was not yet considered a "veteran" player.

The 36-hole final was unique for three reasons: First, because of torrential rains, it took two days to play. Second, it brought together two fellow-Californians, Mickey Wright and myself. Third, I believe we were the youngest finalists in the history of the event at that time.

Mickey and I had opposed each other twice before in California tournaments. Both times I won by a 4 & 2 margin. Little did we know that lightning was going to strike thrice.

Our match was predicted to be very close, which it was on the first 18. I had a 2-up lead at that time, but the next day when we resumed play, things changed drastically. Starting on the 2nd hole, Mickey became erratic with her irons. I ran in some birdies and won six consecutive holes, being 8 up with 10 holes to play. I must admit I got scared and had visions of that margin diminishing: 8, 7, 6, 5, etc. That's actually the way it went. Mickey won four straight holes. The margin had shrunk to 4-up. Now I was REALLY *scared!!*

That important shot I mentioned earlier, happened at the next hole, a long par-3. Mickey bunkered her iron shot, and my four wood landed 2 feet from the hole for a birdie. From then on, I wasn't scared any more. That one shot at that crucial moment was the turning point in my attitude and the match, which concluded on the 34th hole. The winning margin was 4 & 2.

During the presentation ceremonies, while the speeches were going on, I had time to reflect on many earlier thoughts. Would I ever be good enough to be a winner? What about all those long hours of practicing day after day—trying for perfection—having it—and then losing? The gamut of emotions from happiness to heartaches along the way. The drudgery, the blisters, the practice, the mental doubts. . . . Was this moment of success worth it? The answer was forthcoming by the president of the USGA . . . "and now, ladies and gentlemen, I would like to present your National Champion, . . . Miss Barbara Romack."

(s) Barbara Romack

31
Gene Sarazen

Spanning more than fifty years of competitive golf, the venerable Gene Sarazen ranks as the "Dean of Active Champions." The renowned member of the Hall of Fame is only one of four who has won all the four major championships of the world. Gene was a member of the Ryder Cup Team on six occasions from 1927 through 1937. During this period, he lost only one individual match. A master at match play, he won a record of sixty-seven matches in the National PGA Championships.

Eugene (Gene Sarazen) Saraceni, son of a carpenter, rose from oblivion to renown in 1922 when at the youthful age of 20, he won both the U.S. Open and the National PGA Championship. He successfully defended his PGA title in 1923 at New York where he defeated the "Fabulous Haig" on the 38th hole in one of the most thrilling finals of the championship.

Gene scored a most incredible achievement again in 1932 when he won both the U.S. Open Championship and the British Open during the same year. In the former event, he played the last twenty-eight holes in 100 strokes over the rugged Fresh Meadow layout in Flushing, New York. He was also the Leading Money Winner of the Year.

Gene won his third National PGA Championship in 1933 at Milwaukee where his performance of play was most impressive. He won each of his matches by large margins and was never required to go beyond the 15th hole. It was less than two years later when Gene scored the famous double eagle on the 15th at the Masters Tournament which enabled him to tie Craig Wood. After winning the play-off, he became the first and only player at that time to win the titles of the four leading major championships of the world. This was his seventh major victory. In 1940 he made a courageous effort to win his third U.S. Open Championship but the long-hitting Lawson Little defeated him in a play-off over the rain-soaked Canterbury Golf Course in Ohio.

In the Senior ranks, Gene won the PGA Seniors Championship in 1954 and repeated the win again in 1958. Still active in limited competitions, the familiar bronze-faced, stocky veteran of 69, donned in

The immortal professional Gene Sarazen swings on the 1st tee at the Marco Island Country Club, Florida, where he is the Chairman of the Golf Committee. Gene is also the Permanent Chairman of the Tony Lema Memorial Tournament. Tony's statue is seen in the background. Sarazen was the T.V. commentator for Shell's Wonderful World of Golf from 1961 to 1969. The venerable professional won his first major victory, the U.S. Open, in 1922. (Photo by Marco Island Country Club)

Gene Sarazen sinks a final putt for a record 286 to win the U.S. Open Championship at Fresh Meadow Country Club, New York, in 1932. Gene played the last 28 holes in 100 strokes. He had just won the British Open earlier in the year, and he became the second man after Jones to win both the U.S. Open and the British Open during the same year. Ten years earlier, in 1922, this immortal professional, then only 20 years of age, won both the U.S. Open and the National PGA Championship. (Photo by courtesy of Gene's *Thirty Years of Championship Golf,* Prentice-Hall)

The venerable Gene Sarazen and Joseph C. Inman, Jr., walking off the 9th green during the 1st round of the 1970 Masters Tournament. Gene won this event 35 years ago in 1935 with his famed double-eagle. Characteristically donned in his plus-fours, the rapid-playing professional has become an institution in this most colorful event. This was Joseph Jr.'s first appearance in the Masters. He is Gene's junior by some 50 years. (Photo by Nevin H. Gibson)

his characteristic plus fours, marked his 32nd appearance in the 1971 Masters Tournament, the same event he won thirty-five years ago in his very first attempt. He is indeed one of our true immortal golfers of the world.

Gene Sarazen quotes his greatest moment in golf:

First, winning the American Open at the age of 20, being the youngest player to have ever won it.

Second, winning the PGA the same year, also defeating Walter Hagen for the World's Championship 72 holes, 3–2. (First 36 holes at Oakmont, second 36 holes at Westchester Biltmore.) Next day I was on the operating table for an operation, appendicitis.

Then in 1923, I defeated Hagen in the finals of the PGA at Pelham Country Club, Pelham, New York, on the 38th hole.

Now we get down to my greatest thrill: winning the American and British Open the same year, breaking the record score in both. This was in 1932. Then in 1933, I won the PGA Championship for the third time.

In 1935, I made the famous double eagle to tie Craig Wood, going on to win the Masters. Putting the finishing touches to the Professional Grand Slam, American, British, PGA and the Masters. Fifteen years later Ben Hogan did it by winning the British Open.

Making the double eagle was a great thrill, but in looking back to it, only $750 in prize money. We received $50.00 each for a 36 hole play-off . . . doesn't give you much of a thrill. There were only twenty people that saw that shot—Hagen was my partner and Robert T. Jones, Jr., was one of the twenty sitting on the green.

In 1932, the prize money for the British and American Open was less than $1500, but I would not take a hundred thousand for the title.

1970 marks my 50 years of golf.

(s) Gene Sarazen

32
Sam Snead

"Mr. Corcoran, I'd like for you to tell 'em I'm from the Greenbrier Hotel in White Sulphur Springs, West Virginia, if you don't mind. They pay me forty-five dollars a month to represent 'em." Said Sam Snead to the new PGA Tournament Director at 6:30 A.M. in the hotel lobby at Oakland, California, in 1937. That's how it all started. Both, Samuel Jackson Snead and Freddy Corcoran were two weeks in pursuit of their trials. The Oakland Open was on tap and even the scorekeeper marked "Speed" instead of "Snead." Three days later, when the hillbilly won, every golf fan in the United States had the correct spelling.

The above incident occurred some 35 years ago. Now, the world's greatest natural golf swinger in the history of golf has won well over 100 official PGA tournaments. It would require many pages to record the Slammer's numerous victories. To capsule a portion of his achievement: he has won the Vardon Trophy four times, been a member of nine Ryder Cup Teams and captain twice, was the year's leading money winner three times and has won seven major championships.

Sam Snead's playing ability and his talent to swing the club like no one else, combined with his humorous wit with the hillbilly tinge, has never ceased to amaze his followers. In spite of his rapid rise to fame and wealth, he has retained those genuine qualities in his characteristic way of playing and living. He is Samuel Jackson Snead and he still represents the Greenbrier, after some 35 years. For the same period, this most venerable competitor has been one of golf's greatest ambassadors, not only in the United States, but also abroad. His tremendous contribution to the game of golf is immeasurable. His book, *The Education of a Golfer*, gives an outstanding account of his career and gives a true conception of Sam Snead.

Sam's golfing record has one blemish. He has never won the U.S. Open Championship. In his very first attempt in 1937, he came close but Ralph Guldahl established a record and Sam was second, the same position he has earned on five occasions. The major victories which Sam has won include: three Masters titles, three National PGA Championships and one British Open.

The smiling Samuel Jackson Snead has every reason to be. The "Slammer," possessing the greatest swing in the game, has won over 100 PGA events, including seven major titles and countless other awards. Sam, the pro at the Greenbrier in West Virginia during the 1930's, received $45 per month when he went on the Tour. This immortal professional still represents the fabulous Greenbrier, but the multi-millionaire now selects his own schedule of play. (Photo by Wilson)

Sam Snead putts on the 9th green during the first day of play in the 1970 Masters Tournament. Sam, a three-time winner of this event (1949, 1952 and 1954), is now making his thirty-first appearance. His victory in 1954, after a play-off with Ben Hogan, was one of the most spectacular matches in the history of the Masters. (Photo by Nevin H. Gibson)

One of his most dramatic victories occurred in 1954 when he won the play-off against Ben Hogan for the prestigious title of the Masters Tournament, which was one of the most publicized duels in the history of golf.

The following is a narrative of Sam Snead's greatest moment in golf:

I am sure the greatest moment in my career was winning the National PGA Championship in 1942. This being my first major victory and under the circumstances of how I was able to play when it appeared improbable made this victory more important.

I had been a professional since 1934 and playing on the tour since 1937. During this five year period, I had won practically everything in sight except a major championship. These victories included: winning some 25 PGA tournaments, being the year's leading money winner, and never worse than third in this department, winning the Vardon Trophy and playing on the U.S. Ryder Cup Team. Yet, no major victories. On five occasions I barely missed winning a major event. In 1937 and 1939, I had the U.S. Open title practically in my hands, but it got away. In 1939 I closed with a 68 for a record 280 in the Masters tournament, then Ralph Guldahl, the unconscious Swede, thirty-threed the back nine for a new 279 record, to win by a single stroke. I was knocked out during the final rounds in two National PGA Championships. During this period the PGA Championship was a week-long grueling match-play event, man against man. In 1938, I lost in the finals to Paul Runyon and again in 1940, I won all my matches during the week only to lose in the finals to Byron Nelson by one down. I had indeed come so close . . . yet so far from winning a major event.

The United States had entered World War II and I was to be inducted into the U.S. Navy on Monday, May 23, 1942, the same day on which the PGA Championship commenced. At this time it did not seem likely that I would have the opportunity to play for years. I called my Draft Board and explained that I had my physical and asked for a week extension, which was granted. I was most anxious to play in this championship which I realized may be the last for a long time to come, if ever.

"Slamming" Sammy Snead, drives from the 1st tee during the third round of the 1971 National PGA Championship at Palm Beach Gardens, Florida. Sam, a three-time winner of this event, won his first 29 years ago at Atlantic City in 1942. According to the venerable professional, this was his greatest moment in golf. (Photo by Nevin H. Gibson)

I had not won a tournament during the early part of the 1942 season, although I was playing well. My first opponent was Sam Byrd, the former baseball player, whom I defeated 7 and 6. Next, I defeated Willie Goggin by 9 and 8, which ended the 18-hole matches. Then in the first 36 hole match, I just defeated Ed Dudley, the smooth-swinging Georgian, on the final hole, by one-up. In the semi-finals, I met and defeated Jimmy Demaret by 3 and 2. I had now reached the finals in the National PGA Championship for the third time.

My final opponent was Jim Turnesa who was playing the very best golf of his career. In reaching the finals, Jim really made the headlines by knocking out a number of the big favorites. He started by defeating E. J. Harrison by 6 and 5, then Harold "Jug" McSpaden by 7 and 5. Then in the quarter-finals, he defeated Ben Hogan, who for two years was the leading money winner and the Vardon Trophy holder, by 2 and 1. Then in the semi-finals, he had the audacity to defeat Lord Byron Nelson, who among other things was the reigning Masters Champion, on the 37th hole. This was the man I was to play in the 36-hole finals. Naturally, I wondered, would I be defeated for the third time? Would I overcome this major championship jinx? I did have one thing in my favor which was the fact that I had defeated Jim in the last PGA Championship during the third round. Although this was only a psychological factor, at times such an advantage can be most important in golf.

Without a resume of a hole-by-hole description of the match, I did defeat Jim in the 36-hole grind by 3 and 2 to win my first major championship. The victory of that final round on May 31, 1942, was indeed my greatest moment in golf.

(s) Sam Snead

33
Dave Stockton

Although Dave Stockton's father was a golf pro, the personable young-ster played the game seldom until he was 17. Young Dave worked in a lumber yard each summer until his father, Gail, gave him a free hand to compete in as many tournaments as he wished.

Stockton played well enough to earn a golf scholarship to the University of Southern California. He graduated in 1964 with a degree in business management.

Dave joined the 1964 Tour with a realistic viewpoint: "I didn't expect to win, but I knew I could make a good living because I'm a good mental player and I think well on the course."

Stockton also proved to be an accurate hitter of the ball and an exceptional putter. After two "learning years" on the Tour, he won the prestigious Colonial National Invitational in 1967. He added two more victories in 1968 and earned $100,432.

Victories and experience have not changed Stockton. He missed his monetary goal in 1969. It was an "off year" for Dave on the greens. Many times he hit 16 and 17 greens a round in regulation strokes or better, but—"I took 33 and 34 putts a round too often," he recalls. However, in unofficial earnings, Dave reaped a great harvest when he and fellow-Californian, Al Geiberger, teamed together and won the televised CBS Golf Classic over the rugged Firestone Course in Akron, Ohio. Dave and Al had won the 1967 Golf Classic and successfully defended in 1968. They won a record of ten straight victories before they bowed in defeat in the semifinals during the third consecutive year.

Perhaps because Stockton's name had not been in the headlines as a tournament winner since the 1968 Milwaukee Open, Dave's reputation as a fine, all-around player was not as widely known as it might have been. At any rate, after he shared the second round lead of the 1970 PGA Championship with Larry Hinson, a Tulsa newspaper headlined the story, "Unknowns lead PGA." "I was a little hurt by that," Dave admitted later, but it gave me something to work for." After the third round, Stockton was the lone leader and, in a typically-tempered wise-crack, he said to the newsmen: "Make it partially unknown instead of

Dave Stockton hits his approach shot to the 18th green of the Southern Hills Country Club at Tulsa, en route to his victory at the 1970 National PGA Championship. It was Dave's first major title. One would think this was Dave's greatest moment in golf, but Dave selects his victory of winning the Colonial National, his first Tour victory, as his greatest moment. (Photo by Nevin H. Gibson)

unknown." After winning the title, Stockton was "known," the press agreed, and Dave was happy with his victory. "The PGA Championship is a title that puts a golfer's mind at ease," he said, and added: "Now I know I won't have to finish in the top 60 each year to have an exemption into tournaments. I've got an exemption now for 10 years. I think you'll see a lot of me in the next ten years."

Now that Dave has won his first major title, he can eye the others with more confidence. He said: "I very definitely want to win as many of the big championships as possible. I don't think I'm any different from anybody else on the Tour in that regard."

Typical of his modesty, Dave makes little fuss of his younger years of his family heritage. He is a direct descendent of Richard Stockton, who signed the Declaration of Independence for New Jersey.

As a boy, Dave was well on his way to becoming an all-around athlete but at 15, he cracked six vertebrae in his back while surfing. That ended his participation in sports for some months. His work in the lumber yard during summers while he attended high school helped to strengthen his back. When he was 17, Dave started to play regularly. He became an active amateur golfer and eventually won 14 tournaments, some of the same which his father had once won. And, like his dad, Dave attended the University of Southern California. He captained the golf team and gained All-American ranking just as his father had. Over the years, Gail Stockton was Dave's only teacher and the younger Stockton is thankful. He has often said: "Everything my Dad told me has been right."

In 1970 Dave earned $108,564 in Official PGA winnings. His scoring average was 71.4. In 1971, Stockton earned 181.450 Ryder Cup Points and was selected to play on the U.S. Ryder Cup Team.

Dave Stockton relates his greatest moment in golf:

Many people think that when I won the National PGA Championship it was my greatest moment in golf. But to be sure, my greatest moment was winning my first Tour victory on May 21, 1967. This was the Colonial National Invitational over the rugged par-70, 7,142-yard Colonial Course.

Dave Stockton tees off in the first round of the 1971 National PGA Championship at Palm Beach Gardens, Florida, in defense of the title he won in 1970 at Tulsa. Gary Player, also a previous winner, looks on. (Photo by Nevin H. Gibson)

I started with a most brilliant 65 and followed this with a 66 for a 36-hole record score of 131. I was most confident and quite proud of this score because it broke Hogan's record of 135. Then—that third round—I soared to a most horrible 74. It really terrified me and I started thinking in a negative trance of how I may lose. After leading with a record score, I was now tied with Tom Weiskopf. Later I saw Ben Hogan and I'm sure he surmised my feelings, for he stated: "Don't let this bad round bother you, you're playing well." Mr. Hogan is not too talkative and when he does speak, everyone listens. This cheered me up most tremendously and gave me food for thought, and made me think in a positive sense. When I saw my pairing with Charles Coody and George Archer, I figured this was a break.

Colonial impressed me as a difficult course but very fair. It is a "placement course." My father told me if I could get six birdies without any mistakes, I could win the tournament.

In the final round I birdied the ninth hole which made me even par. Then I bogied two out of the next three holes. Again, that negative thinking momentarily returned but I was still near the lead and I recomposed myself and settled down to play.

I parred 13, 14 and 15. On the 16th I missed the green but made an excellent recovery within six inches of the hole and got my par. On the 17th, I hit to the right. I shall never forget—it left me with a very difficult shot to the green. This shot required a high loft to carry over a group of tall trees and if I failed, the ball would drop into a hazard and cost me a possible double-bogey. Finally, I decided on an eight iron and I produced one of my greatest shots. The ball followed the contour of the trees on the upward flight and cleared less than three feet and split the pin, stopping twelve feet from the hole. I two-putted for my par. I knew then that I had a three shot lead. On the 18th 430-yard hole, I hit an excellent tee shot but it hit Coody's ball on the fly. Instead of having a seven iron to the green, I had a four iron. I buried my approach shot in the right bunker. I blasted out almost in the water on the other side of the green. I putted short within four feet of the hole and I thought then I had the tournament won and I walked over to my bag, happy as hell. Then, it occurred to me, if Coody should sink his 20–25 foot putt I would have to sink in order to win. The tide of the game can change in seconds. I almost had a heart attack. However, Coody missed and I was relieved and so elated. I knew I could two-putt and still win. What a feeling. Then I tapped in my four-footer for the victory. My winning total 278 was the only score below par. It was my first championship and indeed my greatest moment in golf.

(s) Dave Stockton

34
Bob Toski

Robert J. Toski is currently known in this era of our time as one of golf's leading television reporters. Not only is Bob renowned in the field of televising golf, but he is one of the most outstanding analysts of the game. A native of Massachusetts, he has been seen on Hughes's network, bringing the live action of many of the top tournaments to golf fans throughout the Nation. He is indeed one of the most respected golf teachers and is consulted by many touring professionals when they are having difficulties with their game. Most recently he assisted the outstanding youthful professional Tony Jacklin from England. Tony has since won the two most prestigious tournaments in the world, the British Open Championship and the U.S. Open Championship. Bob Toski's services are also in great demand at golf clinics and for other personal appearances. His warm personality makes him one of golf's finest goodwill ambassadors.

While he no longer plays the tour events regularly, Bob placed second in the 1968 Florida Open, dropping the play-off on the first extra hole. Yet, Bob was "King of the Hill" in 1954 when he outshot the world's best to win the World's Championship at Chicago's Tam O'Shanter Country Club. He won the $50 grand first prize and led all PGA money winners that year. He also won the Baton Rouge Open, the Azalea Open and the Eastern Open (which was Bob's greatest year). The year before, he captured the Havana Invitational and the Insurance City Open. In 1960, after semi-retirement from the touring ranks, he ventured into the Caribbean tour and placed third in both the Jamaica Open and the Maracaibo Open. During the same year, he also played in numerous exhibitions in Europe at military installations to accommodate and raise the morale of our servicemen.

Apart from his generosity of donating his services wherever and whenever required, Bob Toski has made other contributions to golf. Perhaps one of the most outstanding was when the diminutive 5 foot 8 inch, 127 pounder, competed with and defeated the burly giants of the game. He proved beyond doubt that winning golf is not discriminative of size or weight, but can be equally played and rewarding to all.

A close-up of the personable Bob Toski as he is seen on the television screens throughout the nation. The diminutive 5′ 8″, 127-pounder competed with and defeated the burly giants of the game back in 1954 when he was the "King of the Hill." Not only one of golf's best announcers, Bob is also one of the best analysts in the game. (Photo by MacGregor)

His outstanding achievements have convinced and inspired thousands to pursue and play the game which has not only been healthy for the participants, but to the game of golf as well.

Bob is also on the Professional Panel for the *Golf Digest* magazine and is on the Advisory Staff of the MacGregor Golf Company.

Bob Toski quotes his greatest moment in golf:

Many people consider my winning the World's Championship as my greatest achievement. This being the first fifty thousand dollar first prize in golf. The tournament that really had a great impact on my future was the winning of the Havana Invitational Tournament in December of 1953, a week before my marriage to Jacqueline Stewart. I was desperate, nearly broke, and my bride-to-be had arrived in

Havana during mid-week to watch me play in this event before our marriage in Coral Gables. I had led the tournament for three days and the pressure was really beginning to tell in the final nine of the tournament. I was playing in the final threesome with Walter Burkemo and Pete Cooper—all three needed a birdie-three on the final hole to break what would be a five-way tie. Fred Haas and Al Besselink had already completed their round and were tied for the lead in the club house. It was up to one of us to birdie the final hole for the championship. Cooper and Burkemo hit fine drives on this narrow dog-leg eighteenth hole with out-of-bounds to the left. My drive was pushed to the adjoining 17th fairway, and I found myself blocked out by royal palms guarding the entire right side of the fairway to the green. I had only one alternative, that was to strike a low-lofted club between the royal palms, starting the flight of the ball well to the left of the green toward the out-of-bounds area. I selected a #4 iron (about 170 yards from the green— greatest iron shot of my life) and selected the two palms with which to drive the ball between. Being away I had to shoot first. My shot started well left of the green. I could not see the entire flight of the ball because the tall royal palms blocked out my view. There was a tremendous roar. People started running down the fairway toward me waving their hands and showing me the approximate distance the ball had stopped from the cup—2 feet below the hole, when I finally arrived at the green. Burkemo and Cooper two-putted from birdie distance and I topped my 2-footer in to break the possible five-way tie for the championship.

I walked over to my fiancee and embraced her with a great feeling of security and confidence. You see it was that money that we got married on and from there my career began to blossom. I had told her mother I had five thousand in the bank. I had about five dollars. Winning is easy when financial security is apparent. Winning when you're broke is a tremendous task. Adversity builds character. This is why this championship will stand out in my mind as one of the greatest in my career as a tournament player.

(s) Bob Toski

35
Lee Trevino

No one but Lee Trevino could win the U.S. Open Championship as a first tournament victory and not be considered as a flash in the pan or a dark horse winner. Trevino, the swarthy and stocky professional from Dallas with Mexican ancestry, kept the press most thoroughly amused with his witty and humorous personality for over one hour after his 1968 U.S. Open victory in Rochester, New York. An outsider would have thought the entire interview was previously rehearsed and Trevino's victory over the famed Oak Hill course was a staged affair.

The reason Mr. Trevino was not condemned as a dark horse winner, apart from the fact that he out-witted the press, was obviously based on his outstanding performance in the U.S. Open at the Baltusrol Golf Club in Springfield, New Jersey, during the previous year where he showed signs of greatness. The name Trevino, hardly known outside of Texas, was flashed on IBM's scoreboard as the leading contender. Record books were rapidly scanned to find this name. To be sure, there were no such records of Lee Trevino at this time. However, when Lee finished in fifth place to win $6,000, his largest pay check, and ended the year by winning $26,472.92, Lee Trevino was indeed on his way to vie for higher awards.

Lee was not to be denied for his quest to become a great professional golfer. Not only did he succeed so soon, but he attracted a host of most dedicated followers, particularly from the southwest area and his native state of Texas which has produced more great golfers than any other state. Lee's love for the game, his great personality (never without an answer, even to the caddies), his rapid rise from obscurity to renown, and, most important, the way he carries his success, has indeed made a great contribution to golf and Lee Trevino is most definitely a great credit to the game.

Lee proved his 1968 Open victory was no fluke during the same year. He entered the Hawaiian Open although the World Cup Matches in which he was to play followed one week later in Rome, Lee had a special reason to win the Hawaian Open. Ted Makalena of Honolulu and winner of the 1966 Hawaiian Open was Lee's good friend and

Lee Trevino swings from the 4th tee at the Southern Hills Country Club at Tulsa during the third round of the 1970 National PGA Championship. He scored his second consecutive 77 but he came back in the final round with the lowest round of the tournament—65—to salvage a sizeable check. (Photo by Nevin H. Gibson)

Ted died due to an accident two months prior. Lee established a $10,000 trust fund for Ted's son to finish college and Ted's brother, Harry, caddied for Lee. Said Lee, "I have never wanted to win so badly as I did this one." At mid point, Lee was six strokes behind and was suffering from a bad back, injured when he tried to avoid touching his sunburned wife while getting out of bed. "That's what I get for marrying a Scandinavian, this Hawaiian sun would never bother a Mexican," replied Lee. Apparently he was not bothered by the sun nor the six stroke deficit and Lee finished with 65–68 for a 272 total to win by two strokes over George Archer. By the end of the year, Lee was the sixth leading money winner with official earnings of $132,127.32.

In 1969, among other things, Lee won the Tucson Open, was co-winner of the World Cup Matches and ended the year as the seventh leading money winner with official earnings of $112,417.51.

In 1970, in the final round of the Houston International, there was a pairing that had the galleries buzzing with anticipation because the players were direct opposites: Lee Trevino and Ben Hogan. It was the first time that the "Merry Mexican" had been paired with the "Hawk." Each scored a 70 for identical totals of 287. Everyone wanted to know what Hogan would say about Trevino. Hogan was his usual forthright self in answering. "Trevino can play. He knows what he's doing. He maneuvers the ball well. He makes few mistakes. He's an excellent player." That was early May and Hogan's words later proved to be prophetic as Trevino went on to record his most successful year on the Tour. He successfully defended his Tucson Open title after defeating Bob Murphy in a sudden death play-off. A few weeks later, he won the rich National Airlines Open when he defeated Bob Menne in another sudden death play-off. More important, he scored a "statistical slam": he was the year's leading money winner with $157,037, he was the year's leader with Exemption Point Standings with 1,533.1, he won the coveted Vardon Trophy with a scoring average of 70.62, and a few other awards.

In 1971, Trevino's first victory was the Tallahassee Open, which came on the 25th of April, when he won by three strokes with a 15-under par. One month later, he captured the Danny Thomas Memphis Classic with a 268, and on June 13, he lost in a four-way play-off in the Kemper Open at Charlotte, North Carolina, when Tommy Weiskopf birdied the last four holes in the championship proper to tie Trevino, Gary Player and Dale Douglas, and then made his fifth consecutive birdie on the first hole of the playoff to win.

One week later, Lee Trevino came back to achieve his greatest triumph. It was during the longest day of the year, June 21, when Lee and "big" Jack Nicklaus, the two leading money winners of 1971, met on the first tee at 1:45 P.M. to vie in a play-off for the U.S. Open Championship over the famed, rugged Merion Golf Course in Oakmont, Pennsylvania.

The two contestants, both at the peak of their game, had finished the championship proper with identical 280's which set up the play-off for the world's most coveted title.

On the very first hole, Trevino missed his putt for a par and Jack led by a stroke. Then on the second hole, a par-5, up hill, 535-yards in length, Nicklaus hit a tremendous drive and it appeared that the "Golden Bear" was on his way for a third U.S. Open victory.

But those awesome deep traps, referred to as the "white faces of Merion," caught Jack's ball at the second and third hole, and now Trevino suddenly held a two stroke lead. From this point on, Jack played the remaining 15 holes in two under par, in spite of two bogeys. However, the "Super Mex" never relinquished his lead. After a bogey on the first hole, Trevino played the remaining 17 holes in three under par, a most miraculous achievement which gave him a brilliant 68, while Jack scored a 71. It was an extremely tense and dramatic match from the beginning. On the 17 hole, Lee was in the lead by two strokes, but missed the green on the 224-yard, par-3 monster. The tension rose, but a Merion "white face" captured Jack's tee shot and when he failed in his bid for a par, the championship was virtually in Lee's pocket. It was another most sensational playoff in the colorful history of the U.S. Open Championship. Lee Trevino, who had risen from obscurity to win the U.S. Open in 1968, defeated the world's greatest golfer in a man-against-man battle to win his second U.S. Open Championship.

Trevino is happy-go-lucky but there's a serious streak to the former Marine who lived through hard times as a youngster. "I've set up a lifetime goal for myself in golf," explained Lee. "I would like to make a million dollars on the Tour before I'm through. If the good Lord stays with me, I think I can do it." Lee has already earned over $600,000 in official earnings. This is a most tremendous accomplishment, since Lee's career started as recently as 1966—and he earned $600 that year.

Trevino is one of the most candid players on the Tour, a trait which has endeared him to galleries as well as writers. He wisecracks his way around the course. He states, "I love to see people laugh because it makes me feel good. Being on the Tour is real fun for me and I hope I can pass on some of this enjoyment to the people who come out and watch us."

On July 4th, just two weeks after Trevino's victorious play-off against Jack Nicklaus to win his second U.S. Open title, he came from behind once again to tie the leader which set up another play-off battle. On this occasion it was the Canadian Open Championship at Montreal where Art Wall, Jr., led by two strokes and finished with a respectful 69, but the Super Mex came in with a 67 which required a sudden death play-off. But Lee, who graduated from the title of "the Happy Mex" to "the Super Mex" within a short period of weeks by virtue of his most stupendous performance of play, birdied the very first hole for the victory. The Super Mex became the first man in 44 years to win both the U.S. Open and the Canadian Open Championships in the same year. Tommy Armour did it in 1927.

Precisely six days after Lee won the Canadian Open, he captured the British Open Championship. This victory came just nineteen days after he won the U.S. Open Championship. Within four weeks, the Super Mex won two major championships and one semi-major. Lee's 278 score at the Royal Birkdale Golf Club was 14 under par which gave him the victory by one stroke and Byron Nelson described it as the greatest international competition he had ever witnessed. It was inconceivable that Lee could top his 1970 record, but before the end of 1971, the Super Mex won the Sahara Open Tournament which boosted his official earnings to $231,202.97, topping the record established by Billy Casper in 1968. Lee's career earnings of $644,617.25

Lee Trevino hits an approach shot to the 5th green during the dramatic play-off for the 1971 U.S. Open Championship against Jack Nicklaus at the famed Merion Golf Course at Oakmont, Pennsylvania. Trevino was victorious for his second U.S. Open title. Two weeks later, he defeated Art Wall in a play-off for the Canadian Open and then, just six days later, he won the British Open Championship. (Photo by Nevin H. Gibson)

through 1971 placed him ninth among the all-time leading money winners. This is most incredible when you consider the fact that he won only $600 in 1966 and has amassed this record since that period.

Lee Trevino relates his greatest moment in golf:

One's greatest moment in golf is difficult to describe, for it may depend largely on the situation existing at that instant. My greatest moment in golf could have been several years ago on the 18th green in Dallas when I sunk a 12-foot putt to tie the round. Had I missed, I would have lost $35—a sum I did not have in my well-worn jeans.

And my playing partners were not the type who took kindly to a player unable to pay his losses.

However, I guess that in weighing the circumstances and the probable consequences, I would have to say that my greatest moment in golf occurred when I walked off the 12th green during the final round of the 1968 U.S. Open. I had birdied the 11th and 12th holes to go four strokes ahead of Bert Yancey, my playing partner who had been the leader going into the last round. I felt pretty confident against Bert but, I did not know how I stood with Jack Nicklaus who was playing ahead of me. And he is always a threat—cool and tournament-tested. As I left the 12th green, I could hardly wait to get a look at the scoreboard to find how I stood with the "Golden Bear." I looked and saw that I was five strokes in front of him! For a moment my nerve ends stood out so far I was certain I looked like I needed a shave, my stomach had such an empty sensation that I felt my throat had been cut for a week, and my blood pressure jumped 80 points—a remarkable feat considering that my heart had stopped beating! Man, in this one moment I knew that if lightning didn't strike me, I could be the 1968 U.S. Open Champion! By the time I reached the 13th tee my senses had returned to normal and my greatest moment in golf has passed—a fleeting, but unforgettable moment.

(s) Lee Trevino

36
Ken Venturi

"Hey fellows! watch this lad coming down the fairway now wearing the white cap, with the paddle foot walk. I saw him play in California and this kid can play some kind of golf. He is the one to watch," said one serviceman among the three standing on the right of the tenth fairway at the Augusta National Golf Course during the 1956 Masters Tournament. This was the first time I saw Ken Venturi in action. He did play some kind of golf like scoring a 66 in his very first round of the Masters Tournament.

Following this triumphal day of glory, it was inevitable that Ken Venturi would receive many other great moments in golf. But beyond the shining rays of those great honors lurked an evil omen which cast a dark shadow which was to haunt the life of Ken Venturi during the years to follow.

This is the incredible, often tragic saga of a proud, intense man who rose to the heights of glory and vanished to oblivion, then fought a most courageous battle to rise to the zenith of his profession.

From the very depths of an anguished hell, fighting with weapons of a faith and determination, but with the tenacity of a tiger, Ken Venturi staged one of the greatest comebacks in the history of all sports. This story reveals not only his great moments in golf but his most tragic moments as well. The following account is extracted from his great book, most appropriately titled *Comeback: The Ken Venturi Story:*

Clouds hung low over the pines and dogwood at the Augusta National Golf Club, and in the soft Georgia air there was the hint of the rain which had drenched the course the night before. A faceless throng of spectators lined the first tee in a human horseshoe and I felt a pulse hammer in my throat as the voice of the announcer cut through the hum of conversation: "On the tee, Ken Venturi of San Francisco. . . ." I smiled to myself as I bent over to tee up the ball for this four-day race. Before this round was over, I vowed silently, they would be cheering for Ken Venturi—because the kid from California was going to show these folks how the game of golf should be played. Cocky? Maybe so. . . . I didn't feel the slightest

Ken Venturi swings on a practice tee during the 1967 Masters Tournament at the Augusta National Golf Course. Venturi staged one of the greatest comebacks in the history of all sports when he won the U.S. Open Championship in 1964 at Washington, D.C. It was his greatest moment in golf. (Photo by Nevin H. Gibson)

bit nervous. I wanted this Masters Championship, and I craved it so badly that I could taste it.

On the first round I hit 16 greens in regulation and had one-putted eight greens. When the day was over, I had finished one shot in front of Cary Middlecoff, who had carded a 67.

The next day I was paired with Jimmy Demaret, and when I arrived at the course, there was my name at the top of the leader board.

When I holed out on the 18th green, I had shot a 69; my 135 total for the two rounds left me four strokes ahead.

The third round the next day I was paired with Jack Burke . . . To admit that the pressure was finally getting to me would be putting it mildly and when I went through the first nine in forty strokes, I knew that the gallery figured I was really blowing sky high.

As I waited to tee off on the back nine, I gave myself a lecture. It worked because I birdied the 13th, 14th, and 15th and wound up with a 75. Because of the terrific wind, 72 was the best score of the day. Therefore, I retained my four shot lead.

My whole world centered on the tournament and the next day's final round . . . I almost began to feel afraid to tee up the next morning. It was traditional at the Masters that Byron Nelson should play with the leader in the final round. There has been a lot of controversy about why they didn't pair me with Nelson. Nelson had been my tutor and certainly it would have been a great aid to me. One official asked me who I wanted to play with in the final round, not mentioning Nelson to me at all. "How about Sam Snead?" "It would be a real honor to play with Snead," I replied.

It was another windy day. This, and the nervousness I had never known before made me feel as if I wanted to be ill.

A bystander asked, "How does it feel to be the first amateur to win the Masters?"

From that moment on I was walking in a fog, nerves simply palsied. The very first hole was a tipoff of what I had to expect. I knocked the ball over the green, chipped it back, and missed the putt for a bogey . . . Out in 38, I three-putted the 14th and 15th. This meant that I had shot five bogeys in six holes . . . I hit my approach shot on the 18th hole to the green and faced a putt of about 30 feet . . . There was a low, keening moan from the crowd as the ball slid by the hole, and I felt that the whole world had fallen in on me. I had had it won, and I had thrown it away. It had been my championship, and now it had turned into a complete nightmare. I tapped the ball back into the cup for a 38–42—80 and a 290 total which left me one slender, killing stroke behind Jackie Burke, the winner.

"We are very happy that Jackie Burke has won the Masters," I remember Cary Middlecoff saying at the presentation, "and even though young Ken Venturi's heart may be broken, a young heart bleeds easily but mends very fast." . . . It took me more than eight years to mend the young heart that was broken at the Augusta National Golf Club. There is no way in which I can put into words the bitterness and humiliation I felt after losing the Masters . . . Rolling and tossing night after night as I played again and again each shot of that disastrous final round.

My father . . . left me to sweat it out alone in my own fashion . . .

"Dad, I feel like I just want to quit" . . . "Well, you can quit if you want to because it doesn't take any talent. Anybody can quit. That's the easiest thing in the world, son . . . When you lose, all it means is that you have to practice that much harder."

I did just that . . . Back home I went again . . . Preparing now for the U.S. Amateur Championship . . . The tournament was played in Chicago . . . In the first round I met Bob Roos . . . Bob and I played a great deal together at home and I ordinarily gave him two strokes a side and usually beat him in the five-dollar Nassau. . . . He birdied the 18th to beat me one-up.

. . . I began slowly to arrive at my major decision to turn professional . . . First of all I wanted to play a final time in the state amateur . . . So there at Pebble Beach I was 27 strokes under par for the week as once again I defeated Dr. Bud Taylor in the finals 2 and 1. And I had to do it the hard way, because Bud had me two down in the afternoon, going to the sixth hole. But I eagled the sixth hole, parred the seventh, and then birdied the next six holes in a row . . .

I had definitely made up my mind to turn professional . . . The P.G.A. had a ruling that every new professional had to wait six months before he could accept official prize money . . . However, I was able to start in the Bing Crosby-Pro-Amateur because it was not classed as an official money event. . . . I went out and played it from memory, shooting a 69 at Pebble Beach and becoming the low qualifier. In the tournament itself I finished fifth . . . After that I tied for second in the Thunderbird . . . another unofficial event. . . . I was invited to play in the Palm Beach Round Robin . . . The thrill of playing the final day with Sam Snead, Ben Hogan and Doug Ford . . . was a wonderful experience. . . . I finished seventh. . . . Then followed the U.S. Open and I finished fifth.

My first tournament as a full-fledged professional was the Carling Open. . . . I finished fourth and my first official check was $1,450. I noticed how utterly complete my concentration had become. . . . When I hit a pin-splitting approach to the ninth green on the final round . . . "Nice shot, honey," someone said. . . . I looked straight at the speaker and replied: "Thanks, lady" . . . I didn't know until later who it was. Only Conni, my wife . . . I finished 22 under par at St. Paul to score my first tournament victory . . . I was 13 shots under par in the Miller High Life Open and had put together back-to-back victories . . . We drove out the gates . . . Conni, her big eyes shining, and we never stopped giggling all the way home . . . I only played for three and one-half months on tour in 1957, yet I finished as the tenth-leading money winner..

We became regular golf gypsies in 1958, but I never heard of any vagabonds who had it so good. We drove a new Lincoln from tournament to tournament. . . . Late in the year I scored my fourth win by taking the Gleneagles Open. . . . I wound up the year as the third-leading money winner.

The following year, 1959, began in a similarly satisfying fashion. . . . In the Los Angeles Open . . . I eagled both the eighth and ninth holes and played the front nine in 30 strokes. On the back nine, I finished with five threes for a 33 in and a 63 which beat out Wall by two shots . . . for first prize money. . . . Conni was at home during the final months of her pregnancy and I traveled with Bo Wininger. I scored my second victory of the year by winning the Gleneagles Open. . . . After that I went home to be with Conni when the baby was born. . . . After Tim was born I went back on the tour. . . . I wound up tenth on the money-winning list.

Moving into 1960, I had a feeling that I had attained enough experience. . . . I began by winning the Bing Crosby National. . . . Making the usual trek east and south which led to Augusta and the Masters . . . I was taking dead aim on it. . . . In the first round I shot a 73 . . . I did a 69 in the second round . . . In the third round, I picked up another stroke with a 71 . . . Facing the final round I was only one shot back and it quickly became a three-man race among Palmer, me and Dow Finsterwald. My approach shot on the 18th was about 15 feet from the hole . . . Dow holed out for a bogey . . . which left him one stroke behind my two under par 70 and 283 total. . . . At this point there was a roar from the crowd, hailing me as the new Masters champion, because Palmer was even par and needed two birdies to beat me. I was whisked to the press room for interviews, how different from the tearful scene of 1956, and then Cliff Roberts' cottage where there was a mad jam of some 45 sports writers.

Palmer at this time was on the 16th hole, still two shots back as we watched on television. . . . On the 17th hole . . . he knocked home a 52-foot putt for a birdie. . . . Suddenly the room was practically empty . . . everyone had raced to the 18th green. . . . I was sitting there in virtual solitude with Conni . . . someone came and took us to a room where Bobby Jones was watching. . . . Palmer hit his shot on the 18th green to within about eight feet of the hole. . . . I couldn't watch it. . . . I walked out . . . when I heard the roar from thousands of throats. . . . I didn't have to see the putt drop. Palmer had holed his putt for two straight birdies that cost me the Masters, once again, by one shot.

I left Augusta utterly dejected and low in spirit. Yet pulling myself together, I went on to win the Milwaukee Open, my tenth victory as a professional, and finished the year as the second leading money winner. . . . But my most poignant memory was that galling loss in the Masters.

As 1961 began . . . I did not possess the sharpness that is required of a winner. . . . Once the breaks start going against you, it is like a snowball going downhill.

I didn't even figure in the outcome of the Masters, breaking par in only one round . . . eight shots back in a tie for 11th place. This time Gary Player was sitting in the clubhouse just as I had been the year before, in front of the television set . . . and again Arnold Palmer was charging in on the 18th hole. . . . The scenario was just a little different. Against me, Palmer needed a birdie to win. Against Player, he needed only a par to win . . . he took a double bogey . . . to give Player the Masters title. After taking it away from me in 1960 with a couple of miracles, Palmer handed it to Player. . . . Why did it always seem to happen to me? . . . By now the mental torture of Augusta had become an almost impossible burden. Life was to become far more difficult and frenzied for me and mine in the year 1962. . . . Mentally I was in shambles and I started to ease both the

physical aches and worries clouding my mind by having a few drinks.
. . . Palo Alto Hills Country Club notified me that they were firing
me because I didn't spend enough time at the club . . . I was playing
poorly . . . I began to drink more and more . . . The skid downhill
became a precipitous headlong plunge in 1963 . . . Whispers . . .
about my behavior became louder . . . "Venturi is gone. He's all
washed up."

Looking ahead grimly to the approaching year of 1964, I had to ac-
knowledge the ice-cold fact that it was the end of the line . . . I was
almost broke . . . I decided resolutely to stop drinking . . . go to the
practice tee and work as I had never worked before . . . Step by step;
I was like a baby beginning to learn to walk. . . .

The International at San Francisco which, as I look back, might
have been the start in my turning the corner . . . my first official
check of the year and I talked with Father Francis K. Murray . . .
I had met him fleetingly before. . . . This time he walked around with
Conni . . . when I finished playing we chatted for quite a while.
Leaving Conni at home, I went to Pensacola and was encouraged
greatly when I shot a 65 . . . finishing ninth brought me a fine check
. . . on to New York I registered for the Thunderbird. . . . I went
at it hammer, tongs and ice pick . . . I birdied the 17th and parred
the 18th to wrap up third place money . . . I couldn't wait to call
Conni . . . I had to rush to Franklin Hills near Detroit for the
second, or sectional, qualifying round for the U.S. Open . . . I qualified by three shots . . . I called Conni . . . we were on our way to the
United States Open for the first time in four long years. Washington
was sweltering in a smothering heat wave . . . I headed straight for
the Congressional Country Club . . . it was such an inferno that we
had to give up after struggling through 13 holes. When Conni arrived at the airport, her first words were "how do you like the
course?" "I think it is great, right up my alley," I told her enthusiastically.

After two rounds of play, I was six strokes behind and when I
started on that final sultry day which required 36 holes of play . . .
There was a heartening sign on the very first hole . . . I had a nine-
foot putt for a birdie and after I stroked it the ball ran straight to
the hole—hung there for what seemed an eternity. Then as if of its
own volition it plopped into the cup . . . From there on I let it fly and
my card for the front nine read: 334–334–334 . . . it added up to 30
strokes, matching the all-time record. Shimmering heat waves dis-
torted the vision when I drove off on the 10th hole . . . and the humidity . . . the temperature was said to be reaching 115 degrees.
Despite the dizziness—I fashioned a 66 which meant my total was
now 72–70–66—208 and I stood only two shots behind Tommy
Jacobs. . . . Somehow I arrived at my locker . . . someone summoned
a Doctor . . . His name was Dr. John Everett . . . He ordered me to
lie down . . . giving me iced tea loaded with lemon and sugar. "I'd
suggest that you forget about trying to play this afternoon," he
admonished. "If this gets worse," Dr. Everett advised me, "you
might go into convulsions, I'm going with you and I'll have a hypo-
dermic needle ready in case you collapse in the heat." I thought of
Father Murray's letter . . . and made my way out into that terrifying

heat. . . . There was a storm of applause when I walked onto the first tee. . . . Then taking my driver, I cut the heart right out of the fairway with an arrow-straight drive. . . . After that I fought for each step and each breath. . . . Despite that ever more merciless heat and my increasingly more frequent attacks of dizziness, I was only one over par going to the ninth hole. . . . I pitched my third shot about eight feet from the hole . . . the putt broke a good 10 inches, snaked its way and dropped for a birdie-four. That put me out in even par 35. . . . On the tenth hole I had to make a good putt to save my par. . . . When I rolled in a birdie putt on the 13th hole, they really let loose. . . . "Now you have a five shot lead," someone shouted, and it took me completely by surprise. . . . As I walked to the 16th tee, I was moving like a zombie. On the 17th I leaned back in an attempt to get a deep breath of air and I noticed Joe Dey, the executive secretary of the U.S. Golf Association, was watching me closely. Wearily I told him, "Joe you can penalize me two shots for slow play, but I've just got to walk slowly." . . . Joe smiled, "Ken, it's downhill all the way to the 18th, now how about holding that chin up, so that when you come in as a champion you'll look like one." . . . And at long last I stood on the 18th tee. . . . I let it fly down the middle of the fairway. . . . As I walked down to the green . . . the 25,000 people rose to their feet and sent chills racing down my spine with the greatest ovation I've ever heard. . . . I blasted out of the bunker . . . I lined up the putt, stroked it gently and saw it break exactly as I had figured it would, and ran dead center into the cup.

. . . Pandemonium broke loose as I dropped my putter and incredulously said aloud:

"MY GOD, I'VE WON THE OPEN."

Donald "Doc" Giffin, Tour press secretary of the PGA at the time, describes the part he played on that torrid afternoon on the outskirts of D.C.:

He had a damp white towel draped over his head as he sat limply on a stool and slumped against the wall. His face was slack, lined by exhaustion, and his voice was barely above a whisper. He was at the closed end of two rows of lockers in the clubhouse at Congressional, and reporters covering the championship had crowded into the aisle.

When I realized that only the two or three writers closest to him could hear his feeble response to their questions, I squirmed through, plopped on the floor at his feet, and relayed his remarks to the reporters. Looking at him from such close range and listening to his listless voice, I became convinced that, in the shape he was in, Ken Venturi would never even get back onto the course in the oppressive heat of that June 20 in Washington to play the afternoon final round of the 1964 National Open.

When I heard that he had, in fact, managed to tee off a half hour later, I was amazed and willing to believe rumors that came to the press room later that Ken had collapsed.

Then, as his hole-by-hole score crept farther and farther across the huge leader board in the press room, it began to dawn on me that Venturi was not only going to make it around the course but was going to win that major championship. He was going to blot out the memories of previous heart-breaking failures in the big ones and several years of physical adversity and its attendant blows to his morale.

Without question, it was the most emotion-charged day I spent during my years as Tour press secretary.

Doc Giffin
Assistant to Arnold Palmer

37
Art Wall

It is most inconceivable how Art Wall, Jr., could possibly win 21 professional tournaments (12 Official PGA events) after being plagued by a succession of injuries and illness. The quiet and polite Art has indeed amassed an outstanding record in spite of suffering through a kidney ailment, back trouble, a knee injury, an inner-ear infection and a bad elbow.

Art became a professional in 1949 after a most successful venture in the amateur ranks. A native of Honesdale, Pennsylvania, he twice won the Pennsylvania State Amateur Championship while attending Duke University, from where he graduated. He served approximately three years in the Army Air Force during World War II prior to his entrance at Duke.

Art's first professional victory came in the Fort Wayne Open of 1953. He finished with an eagle—birdie to tie Cary Middlecoff and he won the play-off, which was his first of five tournament play-off victories. In the following year, he won the Tournament of Champions. He repeated his Fort Wayne victory in 1956. In 1957 he won the Pensacola Open and in the following year, the Rubber City Open and the Eastern Open, which brought him to his greatest year.

In 1959, Art reaped his greatest harvest in golf. He started by winning the Crosby National, then the Azalea Open, the Masters, and the Buick Open. With these victories, he became the Leading Money Winner of the Year, the winner of the Vardon Trophy Award, and was voted as the PGA Player of the Year.

Subsequent to Art's great year of 1959, he had won the following tournaments: the Canadian Open, twice the Caracas Open, San Diego Open, thrice the Maracaibo Open, Los La Gartos Open, Puerto Rico Open, Mexican Open, and the Insurance City Open.

In addition to these great honors, Art Wall, Jr., holds the world's record for the 38 aces (holes in one) he has made. However, this is a subject he is reluctant to discuss. He shuns this with, "people will think I am prevaricating, so I had rather not talk about them." No one has ever disputed this great achievement. He made his first by sinking a

Art Wall, Jr., practicing at the 1967 World's Carling Championship at Toronto. Art won the Canadian Open at Toronto in 1960 by six strokes with his brilliant 269. July 4, 1971, Art came close to his second victory, but Lee Trevino defeated him in a sudden death play-off by the margin of a birdie to Art's par. Art won the 1959 Masters Tournament when he birdied five of the last six holes. It was his greatest moment in golf. (Photo by Nevin H. Gibson)

seven iron shot when he was 12, and 22 of these aces were made on his home Honesdale course where he played 36 to 54 holes every day as a youngster. He has had two on tour which came in the Texas Open in 1951 and in the San Diego Open of 1959.

Art proved his supremacy on par-3 holes in 1965 when he established a course record of seven under par during the Par-3 Contest at the Masters Tournament. In this event, he scored seven birdie-2's and two par-3's for a score of 20, which still stands today.

Most of Art's great victories occurred in the 1950's, however, he held his own most remarkably among those youthful pro-tigers who joined the tour during the decade of the 1960's. During this period, Art's "Tournament Play Stroke Average" was 71.696 per round. He won 11 tournaments (including those on the Caribbean Tour), was runner-up 14 times and on five occasions, he finished third. This outstanding record is more incredible considering those physical problems which Art endured.

On July 4, 1971, Art came within a whisker of capturing his second Canadian Open Championship. Art had won the Canadian Open in 1960 at Toronto where he scored 66–67–67–69 for a 269 total, to win by six strokes. Again, Art finished with a closing 69 but Lee Trevino, playing the very best golf of his career, closed with a 67, which tied Art. Lee, who had just defeated Jack Nicklaus in a play-off for the U.S. Open title two weeks prior, birdied the very first hole to win and Art took the runner-up consolation prize of $17,199.

Art Wall, Jr.'s all-time professional record follows:

MONEY RECORD:

1950—$ 350.00	1961—$19,657.54
1951— 589.66	1962— 21,761.90
1952— 3,730.99	1963— 24,389.14
1953— 10,839.03	1964— 17,756.59
1954— 3,930.75	1965— 9,832.02
1955— 17,250.52	1966— 20,929.33
1956— 9,316.72	1967— 52,803.81
1957— 20,831.72	1968— 39,349.54
1958— 29,841.45	1969— 14,431.00
1959— 53,167.60	1970— 24,922.00
1960— 26,380.33	1971— 54,644.20

TOUR VICTORIES:

1953—Fort Wayne Open. 1954—Tournament of Champions. 1956—Fort Wayne Open. 1957—Pensacola Open. 1958—Rubber City Open. 1959—Crosby National, Azalea Open, Masters, Buick Open. 1960—Canadian Open. 1963—Caracas Open. 1964—San Diego Open, Maracaibo Open, Los Lagartos Open, Puerto Rico Open, Mexican Open.

1965—Maracaibo Open, Panama Open. 1966—Insurance City Open, Maracaibo Open, Caracas Open.

AWARDS:

    PGA Player-of-the-Year Award—1959

    Golf Putter-of-the-Year—1959

From such an array of these outstanding achievements, Art Wall, Jr., tells his greatest moment in golf.

As you probably have surmised, my greatest moment in golf came at Augusta, Georgia, Sunday, April 5, 1959. It was the last round of the Masters that year. I was paired with Julius Boros that day. As we left the number one tee, about six people went along with us up the fairway. At that moment I was six shots behind the leader, Arnold Palmer. My thoughts at that moment were to have a good solid round and to finish well up in the final standings. After going out in two under par 34, I three-putted the 10th for a bogey. I had pars on the 11th and the 12th.

On the 13th tee, I for the first time met Bobby Jones, who was there in a golf cart watching the play of the 12th hole, a very exciting par-3. He mentioned the fact to me that he had heard I was a very good putter and intended to watch me for a couple holes.

On the 13th, I reached this par-five in two shots, but some 80 feet from the cup. I two-putted for a birdie, the second putt hanging on the edge for a moment and then falling into the cup.

I rolled in a 20-foot putt on the 14th for another birdie. On the 15th after a long drive, I hit a 2-iron some 35 feet from the hole. My eagle putt rimmed the cup, but I had made another birdie.

The hole on the par-three 16th was cut in the very left corner of the green. I decided to hit a five iron to the middle of the green and try to make a three and go on to the 17th. I was able to do this and as I walked to the 17th tee, Boros said to me that if I made another birdie I might win the tournament.

Until that moment, I was not sure how I stood with the leaders, as there were not too many leader boards on the course in those years. I promptly birdied #17 with a putt of some twenty-five feet. A putt which went up a slight incline, straightened out and into the cup.

On the final hole I hit what I thought was my best drive of the tournament, possibly some 300 yards long, quite unusual for me. I knew exactly where the pin was on the 18th green because I had checked this out before I teed-off the last round.

I felt now from the information I had received that a par on the 18th would win me the 1959 Masters. Boros and I probably had some thirty to forty thousand spectators watching us play the last hole. From a perfectly positioned drive, I placed my 9-iron some 10 or 11 feet below the hole and cut on the front right side of the green.

Art Wall, Jr., sinks a putt while playing in the Par-3 Contest during the 1970 Masters Tournament. Art holds the all-time record in this contest which he established in 1965 with his winning score of 20. (Photo by Nevin H. Gibson)

After looking the putt over from about every angle possible, I stroked the ball dead-center in the hole for a birdie-three. This was my greatest moment in golf.

I had birdied 5 of the last six holes for a 66. I thought I had won the Masters at that point. However, I had to sweat out Cary Middlecoff, who had made a great eagle on the 15th, as I walked off the 18th green. He needed one birdie and two pars to tie me, but was unable to do so.

Later on when I again was to meet Bobby Jones at the presentation ceremonies, he said, "Young man you sure showed me something out there today."

This day was by far my greatest day in golf.

(s) Art Wall, Jr.

38
Lew Worsham

Lew Worsham rose rapidly to stardom as one of the post-war touring professionals. His first National tour victory was in Atlanta, Georgia, where he won the Atlanta Invitational Golf Classic in 1946.

It was at the St. Louis Country Club, June 14, 1947, when Lew had the most prestigious title tucked neatly away until Sam Snead made an eighteen-foot birdie-putt on the last green which duplicated Lew's 282 score. It was the first time the U.S. Open Championship was televised locally. In the play-off, the eighteenth green was again the venue for drama. Both Lew and Sam were within three feet of the hole and Sam proceeded to putt, but Lew requested a measurement to determine which ball was the furthest from the hole. After this Sam putted first and missed, while Lew's putt found the mark and he won 69 to 70.

Less than three months after his U.S. Open victory, Lew captured the Denver Open title and within a fortnight, he was in Portland playing as a member on the U.S. Ryder Cup team. Lew won his singles match then teamed with the late Ed "Porky" Oliver and defeated Henry Cotton and Art Lees in the doubles by a margin of 10 and 9, which tied the previous record established by Walter Hagen and Denny Shute.

Lew had another great year in 1953 when he commenced by winning the Jacksonville Open. Later, on August 9 to be exact, millions of Americans saw him on television making the most celebrated shot in golfing history on the final hole of the World's Championship at Chicago's Tam O'Shanter Country Club. Needing a birdie-3 to tie Chandler Harper for the $25,000 first prize, Lew hit his drive almost 300 yards down the middle. While a gallery of thousands plus a television audience of millions watched, Lew's wedge shot hit the green, bounced twice and ended up in the cup for an eagle-2 and victory.

Lewis Elmer Worsham, Jr., has two of the finest professional golf jobs in the country. He spends his summers at the famed Oakmont Country Club near Pittsburgh and his winters at Florida's plush Coral Ridge Country Club in Ft. Lauderdale.

Lew relates: "I was never a full time tournament player, although

Lew Worsham poses holding the wedge with which he scored the famous double-eagle on the last hole at the Tam O'Shanter Country Club at Chicago to win the 1953 World's Championship and the $25,000 first prize. It was one of Lew's greatest moments in golf. (Photo by MacGregor)

I played the winter tour for eight years, also the major events in the summer months. The game of golf has been good to me and I hope that I have given something to golf in the way of Junior Programs, charitable exhibitions and benefits, etc."

Lew Worsham quotes his greatest moments in golf:

I have two outstanding memories and it is hard to say which gave me a greater thrill.

The first was tying for the U.S. Open Championship and winning in a very close and exciting play-off. My scores in the four rounds were 70–70–71–71 and a 69 to beat Sam Snead's 70 in the play-off. It was certainly a great thrill to win the "big one," as many very fine players have never been as fortunate.

I had just as great a thrill when I won the George S. May Tam O'Shanter World Event in 1953. This event was the start of the rich tour events that are held today and it was an exciting experience to play in this, which at that time was the richest of all events. I got an even bigger thrill by winning in 1953 because I had fallen apart the last nine holes in 1952.

In August of 1952, I led all the way from the first round on, but drove out-of-bounds on two successive holes and shot a 42 to lose by 4 strokes.

The following year I had a 65 the first round, followed by two mediocre rounds and was not really in contention until the final nine holes. I came to the last hole needing a birdie 3 to tie Chandler Harper. I hit my best and longest drive of the week and had approximately 100 yards to the green, which was guarded by a river in front and trees on either side. As I was the last player in the field to play to the green, I knew what I needed for a tie. I hit a good shot to the last hole with a pitching wedge. Seconds later, the ball rolled and dropped into the cup for an eagle-two and a most thrilling win.

These were my greatest thrills and I don't think I will ever forget them.

(s) Lew Worsham

My good friend, Charlie Chamberlain, Associated Press, Chicago, Illinois, was an eye-witness to Lew Worsham's most historic shot and he quotes the circumstances:

In the 1953 World Championship at Tam O'Shanter—the first time golf had been televised on a major scale—Lew Worsham holed out a 130-yard wedge shot on the 72nd hole for an eagle-2 to win. Worsham was in the last threesome on the course. It was nearly dusk. Chandler Harper, playing just ahead of him, had finished with a brilliant birdie-putt. At the edge of the green he was being congratulated on radio by Jimmy Demaret for winning, and George S. May had the winning check in hand ready for presentation.

While congratulations were going on, Worsham spanked his wedge. The ball was low. It carried over the creek, fronting the green. It hit on the carpet and bounded some 25 to 30 feet into the cup. He admitted afterward that it was a lucky wedge shot. As I recall, Demaret stopped in the middle of his broadcast. Disbelief masked his face. He said: "I'll be damned!" Harper was stunned. Worsham's last shot of the tournament won him the $25,000 first place—$15,000 more than second place.

39
Dudley Wysong, Jr.

Henry "Dudley" Wysong, Jr., born and raised in McKinney, Texas, began setting course records in 1958 when he was only 19. Among his more notable records are a seven under par 65 at the Briarwood Country Club in Tyler, Texas, and an eight under par 63 at the Northwood Country Club in Dallas. He was a member of America's Cup Team in 1961 and was chosen as an alternate on the 1963 Walker Cup Team.

Dudley's bid for the U.S. Amateur title in 1959 at Colorado Springs was unsuccessful when Charlie R. Coe, the defending champion, defeated him in the semi-finals. Again in 1961 at Pebble Beach Golf Links, he reached the finals but "Big" Jack Nicklaus, playing 20 strokes below par for 112 holes, defeated him in the final round for the coveted trophy. In the year following, he won the Athens Invitational and the Briarwood Invitational. It was during this next year, 1963, when Dudley became a professional golfer.

In November of 1965 after starting the Tour in May of 1963, Dudley finished in a tie with Babe Hiskey when both scored identical 278's for the title of the Cajun Classic. However, he was defeated on the second extra hole in the sudden death play-off.

After some three years on the PGA Tour, Dudley fired a brilliant 66 on the final day of the Phoenix Open Championship for his first PGA tournament victory. Trailing by six strokes in the final round, he birdied the last two holes and won by a single stroke. Later in the year, he fired a 66 in the third round of the National PGA Championship over the rugged Firestone course in Akron, Ohio, and finished as runner-up for this most prestigious title. In the following year, Dudley received his greatest thrill when he won the Hawaiian Open after defeating the incomparable Billy Casper on the initial play-off hole.

In 1970, Dudley was elected Director of the Tournament Players Division of the PGA of America for 1970 and 1971. He also became a vice president of the PGA of America in 1971.

H. Dudley Wysong, Jr. quotes his greatest moments in golf:

I have been very fortunate because I have had many great moments in golf. Meeting all the good people I have and seeing many wonderful

Dudley Wysong, Jr., poses with his professional instruments during a PGA event. Dudley, a native of McKinney, Texas, won the Hawaiian Open in 1967 during a strong gale which persisted the entire week. His victory came after a sudden death play-off with Billy Casper. It was one of Dudley's greatest moments in golf. (Photo by MacGregor)

*places are just two of my greatest moments in golf. As for playing
in tournaments, I have had three experiences that I will always
remember.*

*The first of these has to be the Phoenix Open in February of 1966,
when I was fortunate enough to win my first PGA co-sponsored tournament. I did not realize that I had a chance to win the tournament until
the last four holes of the last round, and even birdies on the 17th and
18th holes did not wrap up the victory. There were two players still out
on the course that could tie with me if they could birdie the last hole.
I sure wasn't looking forward to another play-off, since I had lost a
play-off in the Cajun Classic in November 1965. Sitting behind the 18th
green, watching the last group play with two players able to tie my
score, was probably my most anxious moment. Neither player tied me
and I had finally won my first tournament since turning professional
in 1963.*

*My second greatest moment was the third round of the PGA Cham-
pionship in 1966. I played one of the best rounds of golf from tee to
green that I have played on the Tour. That round was not my lowest
round on the Tour by three strokes, but a 66 at Firestone Country Club
in Akron, Ohio, in 1966 was two shots lower than anyone else shot.
This enabled me to finish second in the tournament.*

*My third greatest moment was winning the 1967 Hawaiian Open
after finishing eighth in Minnesota when I was tied for the lead after
three rounds. In Hawaii, the wind had blown very hard all week and
the scores were rather high. I had a one-stroke lead after two rounds
and retained that advantage after the third round. After about 12 holes
of the last round, I thought I had given the tournament away. I could
not get my game going and I was two over par. I made a birdie at the
13th hole and found out two holes later that I still had a one-stroke advantage over the field. When I missed a birdie-putt of about four feet at
number 16, I was a little discouraged. I found out after playing the 17th
hole that I was still one stroke up on Billy Casper, with the par-5 18th
hole left to play. Billy was playing right in front of my group, so I had a
chance to watch him play the hole first. He made a great pitch from left
of the green and a good putt gave him a birdie-four. I had driven the
ball very well, but caught the edge of the rough at the dog-leg. From a
very good lie in the rough, I chose a four wood, trying to reach the
front of the green or just short, since the flag was up front. I had
figured that I was about 290 yards from the center of the green with
the wind blowing across and with me. I looked up and the ball was
going right at the flag. I could not see the ball bounce, but everyone was
yelling "GET UP!" and then yelling "STOP!" The shot ended up over the
green and the best I could do was a par five, tying with Casper after
72 holes.*

The tournament officials took us almost immediately to the 15th hole to start the sudden death play-off. I believe Billy won the toss and drove first; he put the ball in perfect position in the fairway. My drive went right and through the fairway, behind a palm tree and another very large tree by the green. My lie was not very good, as the ball was in a depression in the long grass; I was 165 yards from the flag. I had to aim the ball out-of-bounds and slice it around the two. trees. Do not ask me how it happened, considering the position I was in. I was lucky the ball reacted as it did. The shot stopped at the back of the green about 25 feet behind the pin. I guess Billy Casper, probably the most feared play-off opponent, was as surprised as I was, maybe more. Billy hit his second shot in the left bunker, and two putts later, I had won the play-off on the first extra hole.

(s) H. Dudley Wysong, Jr.